fushigi yûgi™

The Mysterious Play

VOL. 2: ORACLE

Story & Art By

YÛ WATASE

CONTENTS

STORY THUS FAR

Chipper junior-high-school girl Miaka is trying as hard as she can to get into Jonan High School like her mother wants her to. During a study session in the library, Miaka and her best friend, Yui, find a strange book—*The Universe of the Four Gods.* As they start to read the book, they are physically drawn into its universe, a fantasy version of ancient China! After a short adventure in the world of the book, they return to modern-day Tokyo thinking it was only a dream.

Miaka and her mother get into a terrible argument, and Miaka escapes back into the world of the book. There she finds that she is being offered the role of the book's heroine, the young Lady of Legends who will be granted a wish and special powers by the god Suzaku. First she must gather all seven Celestial Warriors of Suzaku. Luckily, she has already found the dashing Tamahome, the sophisticated emperor Hotohori, and the beautiful-but-vindictive Nuriko. Now Hotohori has declared that he will make Miaka his empress, which enrages the love-struck Nuriko. And when Miaka confesses her love for Tamahome, he gives her the brush-off. Miaka swoons and collapses.

The Universe of the Four Gods is based on ancient China, but Japanese pronunciation of Chinese names differs slightly from their Chinese equivalents. Here is a short glossary of the Japanese pronunciation of the Chinese names in this graphic novel:

CHINESE	JAPANESE	PERSON OR PLACE	MEANING
Tai Yi-Jun	Tai Itsukun	An oracle	Preeminent Person
Daichi-San	Daikyokuzan	A mountain	Greatest Mountain
Lai Lai	Nyan Nyan	A servant	Nanny
Hong-Nan	Konan	Southern Kingdom	Crimson South
Qu-Dong	Kutô	Eastern Kingdom	Gathered East

TAMAHOME
A dashing mlser and a Celestial Warrior of Suzaku

MIAKA
A chipper junior-high glutton who is trying to get into the exclusive Jonan High School to please her mother

HOTOHORI
The beautiful emperor of Hong-Nan, and a Celestial Warrior of Suzaku

NURIKO
An amazingly strong prospective bride for Hotohori, and a Celestial Warrior of Suzaku

KEISUKE
Miaka's kind, college-student brother

MIAKA'S MOM
A divorced, single mother who wants her children to receive the best education possible

YUI
Miaka's best friend and a very intelligent girl who is certain to get into Jonan High

CHAPTER SEVEN
THE AIMLESS HEART

MIAKA YŪKI

夕城美朱

M I A K A

- Born in Tokyo. Age: 15.
- Third District Junior High School, 9th Grade, 4th Homeroom, Seat Number 18.
- Residing with her mother and her brother (a college student).
- Height: 5'2", Weight: 106lb. Slightly pudgy.
- (But she manages to avoid getting fat.)
- Hobbies: Reading manga, eating, and baking cookies.
- Personality: Outgoing and optimistic. Amicable with everyone. Tends to be guileless and sentimental. Never suspicious. Naïve, but sometimes she surprises adults with an insightful comment. Can be unassuming. Magnanimous and courageous but somewhat unsophisticated. Seems to give the impression she always needs help so she always seems to have someone looking after her. Believes herself to be considerate.

Flower Circle
Seal of Approval

ハア
ハア
MIAKA ... LOOK HOW SHE SUFFERS!
TAMAHOME! WHAT *HAPPENED* IN THE CITY!?!
!!
FORGIVE ME, YOUR MAJESTY.
YOUR FUTURE MAY DEPEND ON YOUR REPLY!

I'M FALLING IN LOVE WITH YOU!
SHE WAS SURROUNDED BY LOCAL THUGS.
I RESCUED HER.
THAT WAS ALL.
YOUR MAJESTY, HER EMINENCE SEEMS VERY WEAK.
...
SHE IS EXHAUSTED BOTH MENTALLY AND PHYSICALLY. SHE MUST HAVE BEEN UNDER INCREDIBLE STRESS AND FATIGUE.
I BELIEVE THIS CONDITION HAS BEEN BUILDING FOR A WHILE.
PHYSICALLY SHE SHOULD RECOVER, BUT MENTALLY...
YOU'RE SAYING YOU CAN'T DO *ANYTHING!?* THEN WHAT ARE WE...
MO...
MOM ...
KEI... SUKE...

GASP!
MIAKA, YOU WANNA GO BACK HOME, HUH?
...TO YOUR OWN WORLD!
きゅっ
INTO MY CHAMBERS!!
Y-- YES, YOUR MAJES-TY!
YUI...
HAÄGEN DAZS...
THE PARFAITS AT KOJI CORNER...
MOLOZOV'S CHEESECAKE...
TERIYAKI BURGER AT LOTTERIA...
I'M STARVING...
UNBE-LIEV-ABLE...

YOUR MAJESTY, IF WE STUCK HER BACK IN HER OWN WORLD, SHE MIGHT GET BETTER.
BRIEFLY AT LEAST...
I DON'T KNOW WHAT TO DO... MIAKA IS ONLY GETTING WORSE.
YES, PERHAPS.
BUT HOW DO WE FIND A WAY BACK TO HER WORLD?
AH!
TAI YI-JUN.
TAI YI-JUN PROVIDED "THE UNIVERSE OF THE FOUR GODS" TO US...
THAT IS THE PERSON WHO WOULD KNOW HOW TO RETURN MIAKA TO THE OTHER WORLD!

BRING "THE UNIVERSE OF THE FOUR GODS" HERE!
HM ??
MY HEAD IS SPINNING.
HUH?
ハッ
I'M FALLING IN LOVE WITH YOU!
SORRY, BUT I CAN'T SAY THAT I FEEL THE SAME.
I TOLD TAMAHOME...

...AND THEN I GET MY HEART BROKEN THE MOMENT I REALIZE THAT I'M FALLING FOR HIM.
I'M SO *STUPID,* GETTING WORKED UP OVER A CHARACTER IN A BOOK...
HOW AM I SUPPOSED TO FACE TAMAHOME NOW?
MIAKA?
HOTO-HORI.
HOW ARE YOU FEEL-ING?
SNIFF SNIFF
I'M A LITTLE DIZZY BUT OTHERWISE I'M ALL RIGHT.
DON'T WORRY YOURSELF. WE FOUND A WAY TO RETURN YOU TO YOUR WORLD.

YES, WE MUST GO TO WHERE TAI YI-JUN DWELLS.
REALLY !?!
THE SEVEN CONSTEL-LATIONS AND THE PRIESTESS MUST REACH THE MOUNTAIN OF DAICHI-SAN BY THEIR OWN DEVICES.
B-- BUT I THOUGHT YOUR KINGDOM NEEDED ME! WE WERE SUPPOSED TO FIND THE SEVEN...
NO, YOUR WELL-BEING COMES FIRST.
THE JOURNEY WILL BE LONG, BUT I WILL BE BY YOUR SIDE, AS WILL TAMAHOME AND NURIKO. WE'LL CERTAINLY ARRIVE SAFELY.
FORGIVE ME. I PLACED TOO MANY DEMANDS ON YOU.
HOWEVER, PROMISE ME ONE THING...
...THAT AFTER YOU GO BACK TO YOUR WORLD AND REGAIN YOUR HEALTH, YOU WILL RETURN HERE.

TO MY KINGDOM ... ...AND TO ME.
HOTOHORI ...
HE REALLY DOES CARE ABOUT ME.
THAT'S RIGHT. I CAN GO HOME. FORGET ABOUT TAMAHOME.
I'LL HAVE TO APOLOGIZE TO HIM FIRST...
...FOR BEING SUCH A NUISANCE.

IT'S ALL *YOUR* FAULT ANYWAY, FOR DUMPING MIAKA!
YOU IDIOT!
QUIT PLAYING THE *TRAGIC HERO!*
KA-WAM
GURK
SO YOU ARE GOING TO *APOLOGIZE* TO MIAKA WHILE WE'RE ON THE ROAD. THEN I'LL MAKE HIS MAJESTY MINE!
MY PLAN IS BRIL-LIANT!
AT THIS RATE, HIS MAJESTY WILL BE *EVEN MORE* INFATUATED WITH THE TWIT!
WHO DIED AND MADE YOU BOSS?
LEAVE ME ALONE! WHAT'S IT GOT TO DO WITH YOU!?
EVERY-THING!
YOUR JEALOUSY OF THE EMPEROR IS PATHETIC! STOP ACTING LIKE A *WOMAN!*
BE A *MAN* AND TAKE RESPONSIBILITY FOR HER CONDITION!

AND I WAS NEVER JEALOUS !!
SHADDUP! I WAS GONNA APOLOGIZE ANYWAY! I DON'T NEED YOU TO LECTURE ME!
HIT A SORE SPOT, EH?
THREE DAYS LATER ...
さわさわ
どたばた
YOUR MAJESTY, PERHAPS YOUR GUARDS SHOULD ACCOMPANY YOU.
NOT TO WORRY. WE WISH TO INSPECT THE DOMAIN* ON OUR OWN.
* THE EMPEROR'S ROUTINE INSPECTION OF HIS COUNTRY.
BUT YOUR MAJESTY, NO MATTER HOW CASUAL YOUR GARMENTS ARE, YOU ELEGANCE CANNOT BE HIDDEN.
YOU SPEAK THE TRUTH, SO I SHALL NOT CONSIDER IT FLATTERY.
HA HA HA HA HA
WHY YOU...

I COULD DO WITHOUT THE NARCISSISM.
どきぃっ
LUGGAGE
HELP ME!
I CAN'T FACE HIM.
ぷいっ
AARRRGH! QUIT BRINGING DOWN THE PARTY!
ギイイ…

LOOK AFTER THE PALACE WHILE WE'RE ON TOUR.
YES, YOUR MAJESTY.
ガッ
DISGUISED UNTIL WE'RE OUTSIDE THE CITY.
I'VE NEVER RIDDEN A HORSE BEFORE.
I'VE RIDDEN ON KEISUKE'S MOTORCYCLE, THO.
IS THAT SO? I'M GLAD YOU'RE WELL ENOUGH TO WALK AGAIN.
TH-THANKS. I'M SORRY FOR ALL THE TROUBLE I'VE CAUSED.
ACTUALLY, MY FEVER HASN'T GONE DOWN AT ALL.
SWEAT SWEAT SWEAT SWEAT SWEAT SWEAT

I've been a little tired lately. How are you all doing? I've been writing these chat sections for every chapter, but nowadays nobody else is doing them. I thought of quitting, but they told me, "Your fans buy the books to read the chat sections." So I'm stuck and I gotta write them. Sniff, sniff.

From "Prepubescence" on, I've been writing a lot of stuff on manga because I get so many questions from the fans (Everybody wants to become a manga artist!), but I've only been a pro for three years. A real veteran manga artist might say that I'm not telling you the right things. I may talk about drawing or other parts of manga but I'm not the artist I want to be yet. And I can't hide my emotions. Whether I'm angry or happy, it always shows right on my face. ☺☹ And that gets me into trouble.

Suddenly my thoughts have come to a halt. I've decided not to think about this stuff anymore. My readers should be priority No. 1! No more long essays on manga. Besides, I never thought that other artists read these books, but a few other artists told me they did read it! I was super embarrassed. I gotta apologize for my know-it-all lectures. Everybody around me knows that I really have no self-confidence. When this series began, I would look over my drawings and feel sick to my stomach. I'd cry and cry while I continued my work! ☹

...
...
THIS IS AN UNCOMFORTABLE PAUSE.
カッポ
カッポ
GOTTA COME UP WITH SOMETHING TO TALK ABOUT!
TIME TO LIGHTEN THE MOOD!
I'D TALK ABOUT THE RIDE, BUT I'M FEELING HORSE!
GET IT?
カッポ
カッポ
カッポ
WISH I DIDN'T.
!

IT'S GETTING DARK.
WE'LL HAVE TO CAMP OUT HERE TONIGHT.
GOT NO CHOICE.
NOBODY'S KEEPING WATCH.
MY FEVER'S GETTING WORSE.
ハア ハア
MY BODY CAN'T *TAKE* THIS...
MIAKA.
BOING

I'LL BET YOU FEEL AWFUL! HERE'S SOME ADVICE...
WHISPER
WHISPER
WHISPER
THERE'S A HOT SPRING A LITTLE DEEPER IN THE FOREST!
HOT SPRING ??
IT'S SUPPOSED TO HAVE MAGICAL HEALING POWERS.
TAKE A DIP. IT MIGHT HELP YOU FEEL BETTER!
THANKS! HEY, LET'S KEEP THIS FROM THE GUYS!
すかー

DRAGGDRAGG
がし
TWOK
OW!
WHAK
UGH!
THACK
YIIIKES!
WHAT THE HELL ARE YOU DOING!?
BLOOOD PAIN
MESSAGE FROM MIAKA! "I'LL BE WAITING FOR YOU AT THE SPRINGS IN THE FOREST!" ♥
WH-WHY ME!?
MAKE SURE YOU DON'T HUMILIATE HER AGAIN! CIAO!
...

HEY!
THERE IT IS!!
GREAT... NOW I'LL GET BETTER AND THEY'LL ALL STOP WORRYING ABOUT ME.
IT ALWAYS WORKS IN THE OTHER FANTASY BOOKS!
CITY CENTRAL LIBRARY
くらっ

HEY, ARE YOU ALL RIGHT?
I THINK SO... I'VE HAD A HEADACHE FOR A LITTLE WHILE.
MOM AND I WILL FIND MIAKA.
YOU SHOULD GO *HOME.* YOUR EXAMS ARE COMING UP, AND YOU GOTTA TAKE *CARE* OF YOURSELF.
THE LIBRARY CLOSED A WHILE AGO.
I'LL GO LOOK IN SOME OTHER PLACES.
NO! MIAKA'S MY *FRIEND!* I CAN'T GO HOME UNTIL WE FIND HER!
OKAY, NOW ...
パサ

スッ
IT'S GONE!
WHAT IS GOING ON? THAT BLOOD!
THAT WATER!
COULD IT BE CONNECTED TO MIAKA...?
チャポ...
ブク ブク
IT'S LIKE A LUKEWARM SPRING. I FEEL A LITTLE BETTER ALREADY.
TO GO ON A JOURNEY ...
BEE-DEE-DEE

MMBL
GRMBL
I'M NOT GOING CAUSE SHE *ASKED* ME TO... I JUST GOT *NOTHING BETTER* TO DO.
AAAAAAAH!
GET *AWAY* FROM ME!!
S-S-SOME-BODY!

MIAKA!!
THERE'S A *HUGE* SNAKE!
DUCK, MIAKA !!
HAA
YAAAAAH!

ドボーン
ブク ブク
T-T-TAMA-HOME.
しーん
TAMA-HOME !?
TAMA-HOME !?
H-HE *CAN'T* HAVE DROWNED !?
I-IT'S ALL *MY* FAULT ??

WAAAHH
SOBSOB
THE SNAKE ATE TAMA-HOME!!
HE'S PROBABLY BEING TURNED INTO SNAKE DOO-DOO RIGHT NOW!
PLA-SHAM
WAIT'LL I'M DEAD FIRST, HUH!?
T-TAMA-HOME?
DOESN'T REALLY LOOK LIKE A SNAKE TO ME.
ポン
WELL, I'LL BE!
PHEW
HAHAHA
YEAH? YOU'LL BE WHAT!?!
THIS LOG FLOATED UP ALL OF A SUDDEN. THAT'S ALL.
はた
...

OH M'GOD OH M'GOD. I-I-I'M NAKED!!
I... I... I DIDN'T SEE ANYTHING!!
ONLY A LITTLE.
WHATTA LIAR.
NOW'S YOUR CHANCE, MIAKA. YOU CAN APOLOGIZE!
YOU CAN SAY YOU'RE SORRY FOR PUTTING HIM ON THE SPOT!
ドキ ドキ ドキ
しーーん
ドキ ドキ ドキ
THAT YOU WERE ONLY KIDDING.
I'M ...
I'M SORRY!!

WHAT.
SORRY, I DIDN'T MEAN TO SOUND SO NASTY.
IT'S THE FIRST TIME ANYONE'S EVER TOLD ME THEY LOVED ME.
I COULDN'T BELIEVE IT... ...AND I DIDN'T KNOW HOW TO REACT.
FOR SEVENTEEN YEARS, ***MONEY'S*** THE ONLY THING THAT'S EVER BEEN ON MY MIND.
ザザッ
I PROMISE YOU... WE'LL GET YOU TO TAI YI-JUN!
SO YOU JUST THINK ABOUT GETTING ***BETTER.***

TAMA-HOME...
SNAP
KER-THUD
N-NURIKO!
I THOUGHT FOR SURE HE'D TAKE *ADVANTAGE* OF YOU.
DARN!
I GUESS HE'S JUST NOT *EXPERIENCED* ENOUGH.
YOU DIDN'T MEAN ...
THAT !?!

HUUUGG
THANK YOU!!
YOU TRICKED-ED ME...!!
IT'S BECAUSE YOU'RE SO GULLIBLE!
HO HO HO HO HO
H-HEY! LEMME GO! LEMME GO!
ばたばた
STOP IT!!
I'M SO GLAD... I THOUGHT THAT TAMAHOME HATED ME!
CLINGY CLINGY
パラ
HUH?

A-A-AHHHH...
柳
YOU'RE A MAN!!
しーーん
HA
HA HA HA HAAA HA
WELL, NOW THE CAT'S OUT OF THE BAG!!
I'M A MAN. GOTTA PROBLEM WITH THAT?
BOING
THIS ISN'T JUST GENDER-BENDING, IS IT??

I'M BEGINNING TO HAVE MY DOUBTS ABOUT GETTING TO TAI JI-YUN.
I'VE GOT ANOTHER HEADACHE.
TAMAHOME'S GONNA SPAZ.
LOVE CAN TRANSCEND EVERYTHING! EVEN DIFFERENCES IN SEXUAL ORIENTATION. HIS MAJESTY IS PRETTY FEMININE LOOKING ANYWAY. DON'T YOU THINK WE MAKE A NICE COUPLE, MIAKA?
YOU'RE A MAN, BUT YOU'RE IN LOVE WITH HOTOHORI! YOU EVEN *KISSED* TAMAHOME!
LOVE HAS FORCED ME TO STRAY FROM THE PATH OF TRUE MACHO-NESS.
YOU ARE ATTEMPTING TO REACH THE ORACLE, TAI YI-JUN! BUT YOU WILL NOT ARRIVE SO *EASILY!!*
THE PRIES-TESS OF SUZAKU ...

Surprise! Some thoughts on the background music of Fushigi Yūgi...

- Lately I've been receiving tons of tapes. It makes me so happy! (Things like "Romancing Saga," "Nadia of the Mysterious Seas," etc.!) One fan sent me Urusei Yatsura and Ranma (was that really Ranma, it was super dark stuff) material to be set to Fushigi. (Well done. Thank you.)

- I might also recommend the game music for "Romance of the Three Kingdoms II." Its sound combines state of the art technology with ethnic music. It's totally my thing. I bought it immediately because Mr. Mukodani from Cassiopeia composed it. ♥ I like the first song that sounds Chinese but the 11th song, "Chosen no Mai," is pretty too. (Better to listen to it on headphones.) But the 14th song doesn't really work for me. I've been skipping it. Sorry, Mr. Mukodani!
  Also the game music to "Madara." I really like the first song, "Ma Da Ra" (Reminds me of the image of the Suzaku seven stars), and the 2nd song, "Yasuragi no Kimi e" (Comfort in You), reminds me of Miaka. Only 5 songs but that's all right.

- Before we began this series, I heard the theme song "Hitomi no Naka no Far Away" (Far Away in Your Eyes) I think! from "Five Star Stories," (I still haven't seen it.) and it gave me an image idea for this manga. A previous assistant copied "Wo Ai Ni" by 135 for me and I fell in love with it! Another song I love is "Nasuka no Kase" (The Winds of Nasuka)! The voice of that singer sounds as if Tamahome's singing.
  Also Logic System's "To Gen Kyo" (It's a long story so I won't get into how I got hold of it. Maybe I should return it.) The CD cover was modeled after the mountains of Daichi-san! "Coffee Rumba" is on it. Most of the songs are in Chinese ("Rydeen" is sung in Chinese. The lyrics are incredible!) by a woman with lyrics in English, Chinese, and Japanese. I really like "Shanghai Moonlight" (although I haven't seen much of it). It's got a sad, romantic melody with backing vocals singing "sayonara" in Japanese -- way cool. They're also singing "I love you" in Chinese as well. (The Japanese lyrics remind me of Japanese enka though). The first song is in Chinese, and the 11th song is the controversial "Virtual Reality." There are several instrumentals. Check it out if you can.

SO THE LATEST THING IS TECHNO POP, HUH?
HEY, "O," P-MODEL'S REALLY GOOD.

This is a little retro but the lyrics to "China Town" and "China Boy" have been used for "Koi wa Passion" (Love Is Passion). I don't understand the English lyrics to "Adieu et Fortuna" from "Lodoss Wars," but I like it a lot too. → (Sorry if I'm wrong. I'd like to hear this song on a nice system).

CHAPTER EIGHT
A DARK INVITATION

...
THANKS, YUI.
THANKS FOR HELPING ME LOOK FOR MIAKA. I KNOW YOU'RE BUSY STUDYING FOR YOUR ENTRANCE EXAMS.
CITY CENTRAL LIBR
I'VE GOT A FEW MORE PLACES TO CHECK.
AS SOON AS I FIND HER, I'LL LET YOU KNOW.
TAKE CARE.

MIAKA ... ...I WAS *SURE* YOU'D BE AT THE LIBRARY.
CITY
WHERE ARE YOU?
GEEZ, I'M EXHAUST-ED!
WHEN ARE WE GOING TO GET TO DAICHI-SAN MOUNTAIN AND MEET TAI YI-JUN?
I WANNA GO HOME!

I'M SO EXHAUSTED! I'M NOT EVEN HUNGRY.
OOH ...
LIAR! YOU SCARFED EVERYTHING ON THE TABLE!
THAT'S MONEY GOING DOWN YOUR THROAT!
TAKE IT EASY. SHE'S STILL SICK (MORE OR LESS).
HEY, WHERE'S HOTO-HORI?
MMBL MMBL
HE HAS TO HAGGLE EVEN WHEN HE'S NOT PAYING.
OH! YOU MEAN HE'S GONE?
HOTO-HORI!
WHAT ARE YOU DOING OUT HERE? DID YOU FIND A REALLY GOOD FOOD CART?
NO.

YOU'RE ALWAYS SO BUSY AT THE PALACE, HUH?
I SIMPLY DO NOT NORMALLY HAVE THE LEISURE TO VIEW THE LANDSCAPE AROUND ME.
I CAN RELATE. ALL I DID UNTIL I CAME HERE WAS GO TO SCHOOL AND CRAM COURSES DAY AND NIGHT!
MY MOM WANTED IT, BUT IT WAS SO HARD!
YOUR MOTHER, HMM? I INHERITED THE THRONE AT FOURTEEN WHEN MY FATHER PASSED AWAY.
IN ANY CASE, MY MOTHER MADE SURE I BECAME EMPEROR.
YOU COULD SAY I WAS SIMPLY HER PUPPET BUT...
MY MOTHER WAS EXTREMELY AMBITIOUS AND THE METHODS SHE USED...
THE POWER STRUGGLE THAT FOLLOWED WAS HORREN-DOUS.
NO, I CANNOT SAY MORE.

THEN SHE PASSED AWAY, AND SUDDENLY MY WORLD BECAME VIRTUALLY SILENT.
I WAS SURROUNDED BY LOYAL RETAINERS-- MY OWN PEOPLE. BUT I LEARNED HOW LONELY TRUE SOLITUDE CAN BE.
バサ バサ…
I WAS LIKE A BIRD IN A CAGE.
BUT YOU CAN PICK UP AND TAKE OFF, LIKE YOU'RE DOING NOW!
YOU'RE STILL YOUNG! C'MON!
LIKE MIAKA'S SOME KIND OF GRANDMOTHER!
どきっ

YOU'RE SO GOOD TO ME.
YOU ALWAYS ARE!
YOU'RE SO CHEERFUL. SO FREE. SO *WARM*...
ドキ ドキ
NOT AGAIN! DON'T GET SO *WORKED UP,* MIAKA!
ドキ ドキ
I WOULD THAT WE COULD BE LIKE THIS *FOREVER* ...
KA-WUMP
HARD WOOD
WHAT COULD HAVE MADE NURIKO SO UPSET?
GROWLL
CHILL CHILL CHILL
TAMA-HOME ...
TSK!

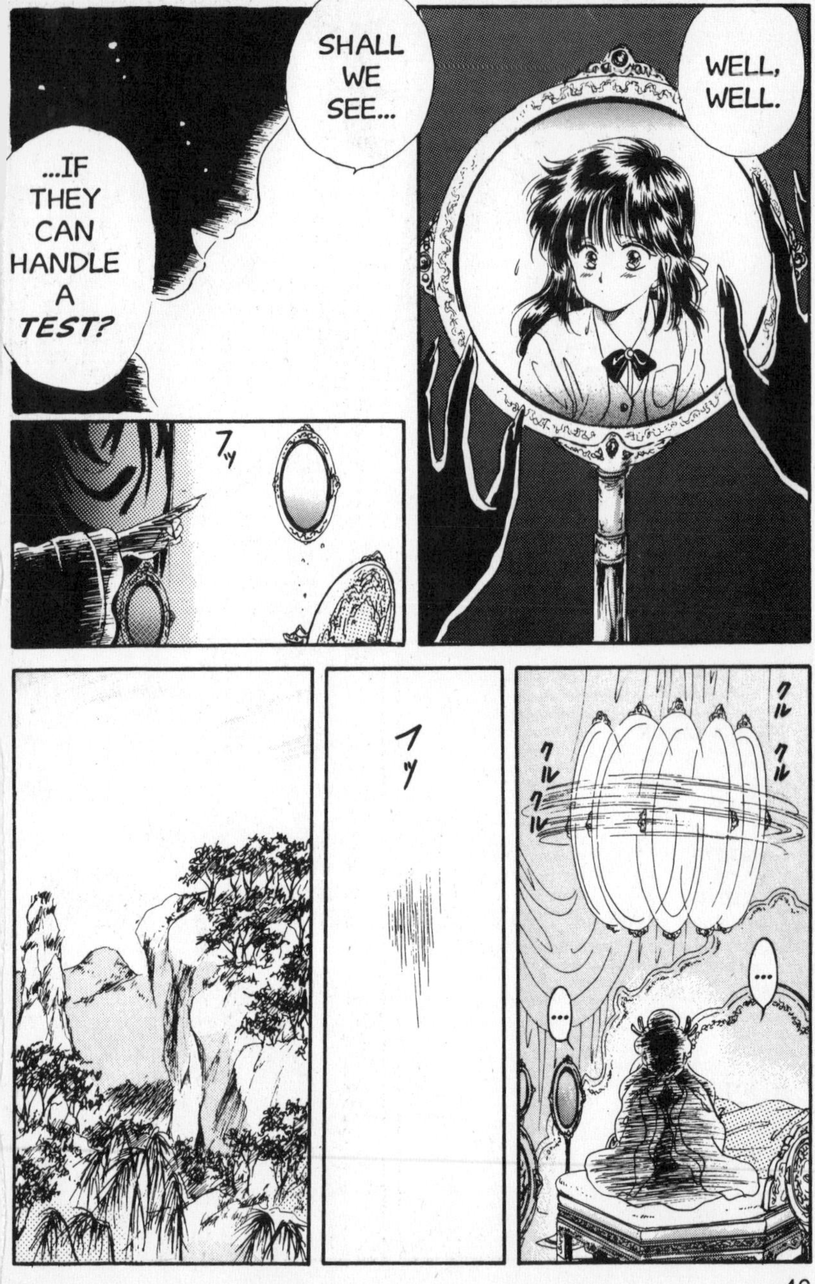
WELL, WELL.
SHALL WE SEE...
...IF THEY CAN HANDLE A TEST?
フッ
クル クル
クル クル
...
...
フッ

カッポカッポ
HEY, MIAKA. QUIT TRYING TO LEAVE US ALL IN THE DUST.
YOU JUST GOT OVER YOUR ILL-NESS.
I'M FINE, I'M FINE.
うん
FWUPP
OOPS.
YOU LOOKED, DIDN'T YOU TAMA-HOME?
DIDN'T SEE A THING.
WHATTA VIEW!
LIAR! LAST TIME YOU SAW ME NAK-ED!
YEAH, WELL, EVEN IF I DID, IT WOULDN'T FAZE ME.
NOW IF YOU WERE SEXIER WITH AN ACTUAL BUST LINE, I MIGHT GET EXCITED.
URRR

POK-KOWW
I HATE YOU!!
ダラダラ
SOMETHIN' I SAID?
はっ
HUH?
HEY, MIAKA! STOP!
DON'T YOU THINK SOMETHING'S ODD, NURIKO?
NOT AT ALL. I THINK WE'RE MADE FOR EACH OTHER. ♥
THAT IS NOT TO WHAT I WAS REFERRING.

THIS MUCH FOG AT NOON IS UNNAT-URAL.
THAT'S TRUE. I GET THE FEELING WE'VE PASSED BY THIS CLEARING BEFORE.
YOUR MAJESTY!
TAMA-HOME! WHERE IS MIAKA?
I LOST HER IN THE FOG, YOUR MAJESTY!
WHY IS TAMAHOME SO *MEAN* SOME-TIMES?
HOTO-HORI IS SO MUCH NICER TO ME.
HOTOHORI IS SO MUCH...

HM? WHERE IS EVERY-ONE?
ZING
WH-- WHAT AN *AMAZING,* MOUTH-WATERING AROMA!!
IT MUST BE *FILET MIGNON* IN CREAM SAUCE...
..COMPLI-MENTED WITH EGETABLE ONSOMMÉ SOUP ND TUNA SALAD!!
A SIDE DISH OF SPAGHETTI IN MEAT SAUCE, AND COMPLETED WITH BITTERSWEET BLUEBERRY SHERBET!!
BUSTLE BUSTLE
WHAT HAPPENED TO YOUR FEVER?
TAH-DAAH!
WHO'D HAVE EXPECTED IT *HERE!*

When I said that I felt sick, I wasn't being modest or begging for sympathy. So don't say, "Oh no, your work is great!!"

Before starting the series, my confidence was at such an all-time low that my stomach really began to ache. My editor told me, "Oh, that. It's an occupational illness." Even now, sometimes when I look at my pages, I just want to tear them to shreds. Or when I'm assigned to do some color pages in the weekly magazine, I ask, "Are you sure you want me to do them?" Or I end up worrying whether they would even put out the first graphic novel. What is wrong with me? My assistant told me I'm weird. Maybe I put down my characters or my work because I lack confidence. By criticizing it, I can be the first to say, "What is this junk?" That's why your letters mean so much to me. I'm so pathetic...

Even when the first graphic novel came out I was more stressed than happy (which has always been the case with my other manga as well). I would worry that someone would pick it up and say, "What is this junk," and toss it away. So I'm happy to hear that people are reading it. I'm happy about the Fushigi Yûgi CDs as well, but I deal with them the same way. Today is June 30th, the day before the release of volume two, so it'll already be out by the time you read this. Ugh, how much longer will this go on?

Oh, yes, thanks to those readers receiving the short "Watase Newsletter" for expressing their gratitude (by fan mail, of course). The reason why I had "Yû" in small letters was that my full name is often mistaken for a boy's name, so just to avoid any misunderstanding with your parents, I figured we could pretend to be friends (which might end up creating further misunderstandings).

The "Post-Recording Anecdotes" in the CD booklet was supposed to be "Recording Anecdotes." Human error. No one seemed to notice anyway.

YOU ARE SUCH A PIG.
YOU MAKE ME ASHAMED OF MYSELF!!
WHAT!?!
WH-- WHAT ARE YOU?
ME? I'M YOU.
I'M YOUR REFLECTION IN THE MIRROR!
YOU'RE ME?
IF I'M ME AND YOU'RE ME...
...THEN I'M YOU...
MIAKA!
?

MIAKA
TAMA-HOME!
ぐしゃ
YOU'RE IN MY *WAY!*
BYE!
EAT TO YOUR HEART'S CONTENT!
LET ME *OUT* OF HERE!
I DON'T THINK SO!
...
I PREFER HOTOHORI. TAMAHOME'S JUST SO COLD!
SO I'LL JUST STAY IN THIS WORLD AND LIVE WITH HOTOHORI *FOREVER.*
ぬりぬり

I DON'T WANT TO GO BACK TO THE REAL WORLD.
WHO'D WANT TO GO BACK TO THOSE AWFUL ENTRANCE EXAMS?
I'LL NEVER GO TO SCHOOL OR CRAM SCHOOL AGAIN!
WAIT! LEMME OUT OF HERE!
NOW IT'S YOUR TURN TO BECOME MY IMAGE AND WATCH ME FROM THE BACK SIDE OF THE MIRROR!
HA HA HA HA HA HA
"NO ONE CAN SEE OR HEAR YOU OUT THERE."
"JUST TRY TO BREAK MY SPELL, MIAKA. IF YOU REALLY ARE THE PRIESTESS OF SUZAKU THAT IS!"

WHO'S THERE !?
SCARF
SCARF
GOBBLE
GOBBLE
GULP
GULP
...
WHO'S THERE!? WHO ARE YOU!?
ぷはっ
DOES *ANYTHING* RUIN YOUR APPETITE!?
MIAKA!
YOU'RE HERE! WHERE *WERE* YOU?
WELL, UM... I FOUND THIS NEAT MIRROR.

WERE YOU WORRIED ABOUT ME, TAMA-HOME?
ドキッ
N-- NOT REALLY.
WHAT'S GOING ON?
STOP THAT! GET *AWAY* FROM TAMAHOME!
I'M RELIEVED YOU ARE UNHARM-ED!
!!
YEP! I'M SORRY, *DARLING.* ♥
HUG
AIEEE!

WHY DON'T YOU *GIVE UP* ON HOTOHORI ALREADY!
I MEAN, YOU'RE A *MAN*, FOR CRISSAKE!
NURIKO, WHAT IS YOUR PROBLEM?
M-MIAKA, HOW *DARE* YOU...
A M-- A M-- A *MAN!?*
TH--THAT'S IMPOSSIBLE!
I THOUGHT *I* WAS THE ONLY MAN ALLOWED TO BE THAT PRETTY.
KRAKKA KRAKKA KRAKKA
HOW *COULD* YOU!
YOU SOLD ME OUT!
YOU'RE SELLING YOURSELF OUT!
NURIKO!!
GULP

THIS ISN'T ...
FORGET ABOUT THAT LOSER... *COME* TO ME, HOTOHORI!
EVERYTHING WILL *FALL APART* AT THIS RATE!!
DOESN'T *ANY-BODY* NOTICE THE TRUTH!?
...
!!
LET'S PICK UP WHERE WE LEFT OFF... AS LONG AS I'M WITH YOU, WHO *NEEDS* MY WORLD?
LET'S FORGET THAT STUPID OLD TAI YI-JUN.
NO!
...

YOU LOVE ME, RIGHT?
AND I LOVE YOU...
IF YOU *DESIRE* ME, TAKE ME!
N-NO.... HOTOHORI!
TAMAHOME!
THAT *ISN'T* ME!

MIAKA !?
GET ME...
... OUT OF HERE !!
"GET ME OUT OF HERE!!"
THAT WAS MIAKA'S VOICE.
CITY CENTRAL LIBRARY
I *THOUGHT* SHE WAS IN THE LIBRARY!

ストッ
たたっ
パアッ
HOLD ON, MIAKA!
WHO IS THAT !?
OH, NO!

NOW, WHO ARE YOU!?
YOU ARE *NOTHING* LIKE THE MIAKA I KNOW.
SHOW ME WHO YOU *ACTUALLY* ARE!
HA HA HA HA HA
PREPARE YOURSELF, TAMAHOME!
WHERE'S THE *REAL* MIAKA!?

RIGHT UNDER YOUR NOSE!
I'M THE VERY IMAGE OF HER. I *AM* MIAKA.
OH--
I DOUBT THAT A *PATHETIC* COLLECTION OF MISFITS LIKE YOU COULD *EVER* REACH TAI YI-JUN.
SO SHE'S ME...
...I HARBOR THOSE HORRIBLE FEELINGS.
ALL THE THINGS SHE SAYS AND DOES ARE THOUGHTS *I'VE* HIDDEN DEEP INSIDE ME!

DON'T BE ABSURD !!
URRGGH!
TAMA-HOME! HOTO-HORI!

A- ALL MY STRENGTH IS...
... FLOWING OUT OF ME.
YOUR *BELOVED* MIAKA IS ON THE OTHER SIDE OF THIS MIRROR.
YOU GIVE YOUR LIVES TO PROTECT MIAKA, RIGHT? SO IT ONLY MAKES SENSE THAT I SHOULD TAKE ALL YOUR STRENGTH FROM YOU.
I *AM* MIAKA, AFTER ALL!
S-- STOP IT!
TRY TO SAVE THEM IF YOU CAN, MISS "PRIESTESS OF SUZAKU."

I GOTTA DO SOME-THING!!
I GOTTA GET RID OF HER SOME-HOW!
SHOW ME, PRIESTESS OF SUZAKU...
SHOW ME WHAT YOU'RE CAPABLE OF!
STOP IT!
M-- MIAKA ...

HA!
SHE'S ME!
IF SHE'S ME...
THEN I HAVE TO...
...GET RID OF *MYSELF.*

PARDON THE PARODY

INCREASING YOUR FUSHIGI YŪGI ENJOYMENT BY 100%!

AIN'T IT AMAZIN...!?

IDEA - K. OF TOKYO (A MANGA ASSISTANT)

BY Y.W. ▶ (A MANGA ARTIST)

CHAPTER NINE
AWAKENING
MEMORIES

LET ME GO !!
CITY CENT
THE LIBRARY'S CLOSED! GO HOME!
MY FRIEND'S STILL INSIDE! SO JUST...
...LET GO OF ME!
KER-THUD KER-WHAM KER-PLUNK
OUCHIE
ぴくっ

!
!!
ARRRGH!!!
I DIDN'T DO NOTHIN' ...!
チャリン

MI-
-AKA?
MY REFLECTION SHOULD JUST DISAPPEAR!
DISAP-PEAR!!
URK
!
GARR --

TAMA-
HOME!

TAMA-HOME!
URRGGH!
ゲボッ
AIN'T SHE CUTE?

I THOUGHT SOMETHING SEEMED FUNNY.
HMPH.
NURIKO!
WHUMP
I'M STUNNED!
FWSSHH
YOU HANDLE A SWORD WELL, YOUR MAJESTY.
CUT THE MELODRAMATICS!
YES, YOUR MAJESTY.
OH!
TAMA-HOME!! ARE YOU ALL RIGHT!?

HM...
BUT NOT SO WELL AS YOU.
...
CAN YOU STAND?
YOUR MAJESTY!
MIAKA !!

MIAKA!
WHAT HAPPENED?
LOOK AT THIS! THE FAKE MIAKA WAS BLEEDING FROM THE SAME SPOT...
GASP
MIAKA DIDN'T DO THIS JUST TO *SAVE* US!?
MIAKA!!
COME ON, MIAKA!!
EVERYONE SOUNDS SO FAR AWAY...
WHAT'S HAPPENED TO ME?
HUH...

WHERE AM I?
OH, NO. I CAN'T DO THIS.
MIAKA!!
AM I GOING TO DIE?
I'VE NEVER SEEN *ANYONE*...
...LIKE THIS GIRL!
YOU TWO, LOOK AWAY!
HUH!?
I'M GOING TO TAKE HER CLOTHES OFF AND BANDAGE HER.
THAT'S RIGHT. I STABBED MYSELF...

YOU GOT YOURSELF PRETTY GOOD THIS TIME!
ビッ
!! THESE WOUNDS ARE HORRIBLE!
WAIT! YOU'RE A MAN TOO!
YES, BUT I HAVE THE SOUL OF A WOMAN!
SPRKL
IS MIAKA GOING TO BE ALL RIGHT?
FORTUNATELY, SHE MISSED HER HEART. BUT IT'LL ALL DEPEND ON HER WILL TO LIVE.
!!

MIAKA!!
OH, NO! THE BLEEDING WON'T STOP!!
IF IT KEEPS UP LIKE THIS...!
IT'S MY FAULT. IF I HADN'T BEEN SO COLD, THIS WOULDN'T HAVE HAPPENED!
WAKE UP!!
MIAKA, DON'T *LEAVE* US!!

SHE'S GETTING PALE!
NURIKO, WHAT CAN... WHAT CAN WE DO!?
IF WE COULD GIVE HER BLOOD... BUT WE CAN'T! WE DON'T HAVE THE INSTRUMENTS TO OPERATE!
BLOOD !?
I DON'T HEAR A THING...
NOBODY'S HERE.
AM I GOING TO DIE?
ZING!

I just want you to know, it's not true! I heard there's been some controversy saying "Watase's a sex fiend! ...(unbelievable!) Let's just get this straight! The only comic that comes close to being sexy is "Prepubescence." Quite a few readers told me they had dreams about Asuka and the other characters, so I guess the story left a pretty strong impression. On page 141 of volume 7 of "Prepubescence," I wrote, "I wouldn't want people to think I'm turning into a perv," I didn't mean I was put out by it, I only meant people shouldn't get worked up over this stuff. Teenage girls might get excited and embarrassed and squeal "Oh m'god! She's so dirty," but to girls in their twenties, talking about this kind of stuff is so common, it's nothing special. So it's not a matter of being a "perv" or not. So this stuff might shock teenage girls You're so young. (Where am I going with this thought?) If bed scenes are necessary then I have no problem depicting them to the extent that they won't cause any major controversy. But I hate gratuitous sex scenes. Now that the plot is thickening I might have to include a sex scene or two in a serious context. (What? You're happy to hear that?) The characters are developing in volume 1, and in volume 2 they're finally getting to know each other.

But if the sales fall off, I'll have to start drawing autobiographical manga (What the heck would I write about!?). There was quite a bit of...that in the "Prepubescence" side story ııı but the average age of the readers is pretty high, so I'll be all right. In any case, those scenes represent an expression of love so I don't think they're bad at all. I do think that gratuitous, superficial love scenes might have a bad effect on the reader. What am I talking about!?

Watase: artist for the boys' comic, Shônen Perv.

YOU'RE GOING TO PASS THE TEST FOR JONAN HIGH SCHOOL!
DON'T YOU DARE HUMIL-IATE YOUR MOTHER!
M-- MOM!
YOU NEVER LISTEN TO WHAT I SAY!
I HOPE YOU NEVER COME HOME!!
MOM !!
YŪKI! YOU'RE THE WORST FLUNKOUT I'VE EVER SEEN!
MY CRAM SCHOOL TEACHER !!
THWAK
HARD LOVE
OWW

THERE ISN'T ONE HIGH SCHOOL THAT WILL ACCEPT YOU!
YOU MIGHT AS WELL QUIT RIGHT NOW!
YOU SHOULD QUIT!
YOU'D EVEN FAIL REMEDIAL CLASSES!
NO !!
THAT'S RIGHT ...
ハァ
I'M BETTER OFF DEAD!
ハァ
ハァ
ハァ
I'M A FAILURE, JUST GETTING IN EVERYBODY'S WAY.
I DESERVE TO DIE.

IF I GO OVER THERE...
...I CAN FINALLY TAKE IT EASY.
MIAKA !!
ハッ
CITY CENTRAL LIBRARY
MIAKA?
WHERE ARE YOU?
ズルッ
ズルッ

ズル
MIAKA!
Y-- *YUI!*
YOU *ARE* MIAKA! WHERE ARE YOU!? WHAT ARE YOU DOING!?
MIAKA!
YUI! I'M INSIDE THE BOOK!
THE UNIVERSE OF THE FOUR GODS JAPANESE TRANSLATION BY EINOSUKE OKUDA
THE *BOOK!?* YOU MEAN THAT...
THAT'S RIGHT! "THE UNIVERSE OF THE FOUR GODS!" WE BOTH SAW IT! I'M CLOSED UP INSIDE.

ハァハァ
I THOUGHT THAT MIGHT BE IT...
YOU'RE WOUNDED PRETTY BADLY, HUH?
ズルッ
HOW DID YOU KNOW?
I JUST KNOW... HOLD ON. I'LL BE THERE IN A SECOND...
NO, YUI, YOU CAN'T! I DON'T THINK I CAN COME BACK ANYMORE ...
MIAKA!
WHY!? HEY, DON'T GIVE UP!
COME BACK HOME!!

RESTRICTED PRIVATE LIBRARY
BUT ...
ズルッ
I'LL GET YOU OUT OF THE BOOK SO...
...DON'T YOU *DARE* GIVE UP, MIAKA!!
YUI ...
ポッ

YOU CAN'T DIE!!
DON'T GIVE UP, MIAKA!
AMAHOME?
OTOHORI?

IF YOU NEED BLOOD, YOU CAN HAVE EVERY-THING I'VE GOT!!
IF THAT WOULD SAVE YOU!
I'LL EXCHANGE MY LIFE FOR YOURS!!
ONLY FOR YOU!!
I-- I...

I *WON'T* GIVE UP...
MIAKA!
ボタボタッ
MIAKA!
I'M *NOT* GONNA DIE!
ぴくんっ
HER BLEEDING...
IT'S STOPPED!

AM I... STILL ALIVE?
TAMAHOME ...? HOTOHORI, NURIKO...
MIAKA !!
OUCH.
YOU LITTLE JERK. WE WERE *WORRIED* ABOUT YOU!
I AM OVER-JOYED.
...
C'MON!
BWAAHH
YOU REALLY ARE TAMA-HOME!
HA HA

I NEVER THOUGHT FOR A SECOND THAT A STUPID, OVERLY OPTIMISTIC FOOD-MONGER LIKE YOU WOULD DIE!
NYAH NYAH
NYAH NYAH
OH, SHRIVEL AND DIE, NURIKO.
IT WAS REALLY DARK. THEN I FOUND THIS BEAUTIFUL PLACE.
BUT EVERYONE WAS CALLING FOR ME.
SO I DIDN'T GO.
THANK YOU.
WHA...?

WHAT THE --?
THE VIEW'S COMPLETELY DIFFERENT!
YOUR FEELINGS TOWARD ONE ANOTHER ARE NOW CLEAR.
YOU HAVE ARRIVED AT THE LAND OF MY HOME.
NO WAY! THIS IS HEAVEN?
YER KIDDIN', RIGHT?
SKRCH SKRCH
OH!
NO, THIS IS...
... DAICHI-SAN MOUNTAIN !!

ス…
WELCOME, MIAKA.
TAI YI-JUN!
I SHALL NOW INFORM YOU AND YOUR THREE CELESTIAL WARRIORS ...
...OF THE METHOD TO RETURN YOU TO YOUR WORLD.

WHAT'LL I DO IF EVERYONE LIKES THIS BETTER THAN THE ORIGINAL?
PARDON THE PARODY
IDEA - Y.M.
YOU CAN'T DIE!!
DON'T GIVE UP, MIAKA!
TAMAHOME? HOTOHORI!?
しっ
IF YOU NEED BLOOD, I'LL GIVE YOU *HIS*!
が
HEY!
YOU ARE *SUCH* A CREEP!
AND ONE MUST WATCH *YOU* EVERY MOMENT!
SHE'S DEAD, GUYS.

CHAPTER TEN
COME BACK HOME

THE W--
THE WICKED WITCH OF THE EAST!!
HMPH!
WATCH YOUR *MOUTH,* CHICKIE !!

SO-- SO YOU'RE REALLY TAI YI-JUN?
THAT'S RIGHT. I'M THE RULER OF THIS WORLD... HOTOHORI! HOW DARE YOU TURN AWAY!?
I CANNOT BEAR UGLINESS!
BE THAT AS IT MAY...
ALL OF YOU ARE ALL QUITE BADLY WOUNDED WITH THE EXCEPTION OF NURIKO!
I WAS TESTING YOU TO SEE HOW MUCH YOU CARED FOR EACH OTHER, BUT I NEVER EXPECTED THIS!
T-TESTING...
MIAKA!
DON'T GET EXCITED! YOU'LL AGGRAVATE YOUR WOUND!
NOTHING ELSE TO BE DONE. I'LL TAKE YOU TO MY PALACE.
WE'LL TALK THERE.
WHOAH!

THIS IS AMAZING ...
WE'RE PERFECTLY SAFE. WE WON'T DROP TO A BLOODY DEATH.

ONLY THE CHOSEN ONES CAN COME TO OR EVEN SEE THIS MOUNTAIN.
HA HA HA..
THOSE WITH EVIL INTENTIONS WILL ONLY FIND A PLAIN HILL.
RESTRICTED PRIVATE LIBRARY
FOUND IT!
四神天地書
パラ…

MIAKA... WHERE ARE YOU?
パラ
...GALLANT YOUNG MAN WHO BORE THE CHARACTER FOR DEMON ON HIS FOREHEAD...
...YOUNG MAN, TAMAHOME, TOOK THE YOUNG LADY'S HAND AND DREW HER FROM THE CROWD...
...TOO CHEAP!" THE YOUNG LADY WAS CERTAIN THIS WAS NO JOKE...
!!
I SEE... SO MIAKA IS THIS "YOUNG LADY."
TAMA-HOME...
OH... SO THAT BOY'S NAME IS TAMA-HOME...

By the way, my profile in "The Watase Newsletter" includes something about my leg size, but that's really my shoe size. I can wear a size 25. 25.5 is a loose fit, but 25 is a little too tight. My shoe size is about average for my height. When I mentioned my age in an earlier chat section, someone said, "So you're 26!" Wrong-o! "Prepubescence" began in December of '90, and I started this serial less than a year later. How could I be 26!? I graduated high school only 4 years ago. sob sob

Oh yeah! Someone from my old high school wrote me! I've had several letters from students there. She's in the Manga Research Club! When I entered high school, I really wished that this club existed! I had no other choice but to join the art club and cinema club. But all they had me doing was ink and paint on Vifam and MinkyMomo cels. I quit both clubs within 6 months. It seems like ages ago. I still remember it clearly though. According to this letter, a teacher I had during my senior year keeps a copy of my manga in his desk! Unbelievable!! I hope he's doing well! I'd never do the chores he assigned, I'd barely pass his math classes. I was a rotten student, but it was a good school. I heard that the name's been changed to "Sakai Girl's High School." I guess all the badges have different designs now. The one thing I didn't like at school was the winter uniform!! I wanted a ribbon or a tie!! (I've graduated so I can criticize them all I want!) Are the uniforms still ugly? Miaka's uniform is a fan favorite because it's cute. I mean, you have to wear your uniform every day. So cute is good. When I was in school, I was so envious of another Sakai school. They were co-ed. What am I trying to say? My teachers were very committed. (It was a private school, so the rules were strict.) Thanks for all your help! I loved my time in junior high and high school. I'd like to go back -- wear my uniform, carry my bag, and joke around with my friends. I'm sure some of you who are still in school say you hate it, but your school days become a great memory.

I FEEL THE SAME PAIN AND SUFFERING MIAKA GOES THROUGH IN THE BOOK.
BUT WHY !?
四神天地書

NOW THEN...
FIRST WE HAVE TO HEAL YOUR WOUNDS.
LAI LAI!
ポウ
PON
ストッ
TREAT THEIR WOUNDS.
わら
わら
YOU A GIRL! PLEASE, THIS WAY!

MISTRESS TAI YI-JUN, PLEASE TREAT TAMAHOME AND HOTOHORI *BEFORE* BOTHERING WITH ME!
THEY RISKED THEIR *LIVES* FOR ME. AND MY WOUNDS AREN'T THAT SERIOUS.
I FIX-HEAL YOU, TOO!
ME? I'M NOT WOUNDED.
MAN
WHAK!
I HEAL YOUR *PERVERSION.*
IN YOUR PRESENT CONDITION, YOU'D *NEVER* MAKE IT BACK TO YOUR WORLD IN ONE PIECE!
IF YOU DON'T SETTLE DOWN AND GET YOURSELF HEALED, YOUR TRIP HOME WILL TAKE FOREVER!
ぬっ
I'D LIKE TO HEAL TAI YI-JUN FACE...
ばばっ
NOPE. I HEAL YOU.
I DISINFECT YOU!
AIEE!

YOU DON'T HAVE AN OUNCE OF STRENGTH LEFT!
AN ASHEN-FACED GIRL LIKE YOU HAS NO *RIGHT* TO ASK.
BUT I HAVE ENTRANCE EXAMS!
I *HAVE* TO GO BACK... SO PLEASE TELL ME *HOW.*
GIVE OUR BLOOD TO MIAKA!
THEN PLEASE, LET HER HAVE *OUR* BLOOD, TAI YI-JUN!

OH! OH, NO! YOU CAN'T!
I COULD, I SUPPOSE. BUT YOUR STRENGTH WILL BE GREATLY DIMINISHED.
EXACTLY MY DESIRE.
WHAT GOOD'S MY BLOOD TO ME WHEN IT'S JUST DRIPPING ON THE GROUND?
TAMAHOME... HOTOHORI...
VERY WELL.
HEY!
ポゥ…

WHA
TAMA-HOME, HOTO-HORI...
I WILL NOW USE MY WILL TO PASS YOUR BLOOD FROM YOUR BUBBLES INTO MIAKA'S WOUND, AND INTO HER BODY.
IT WILL BE PAINFUL. *BEAR* IT!

TAMA HOME HOTO HORI
I'M OKAY! DON'T DO IT!
OH ...
IT'S HOT!

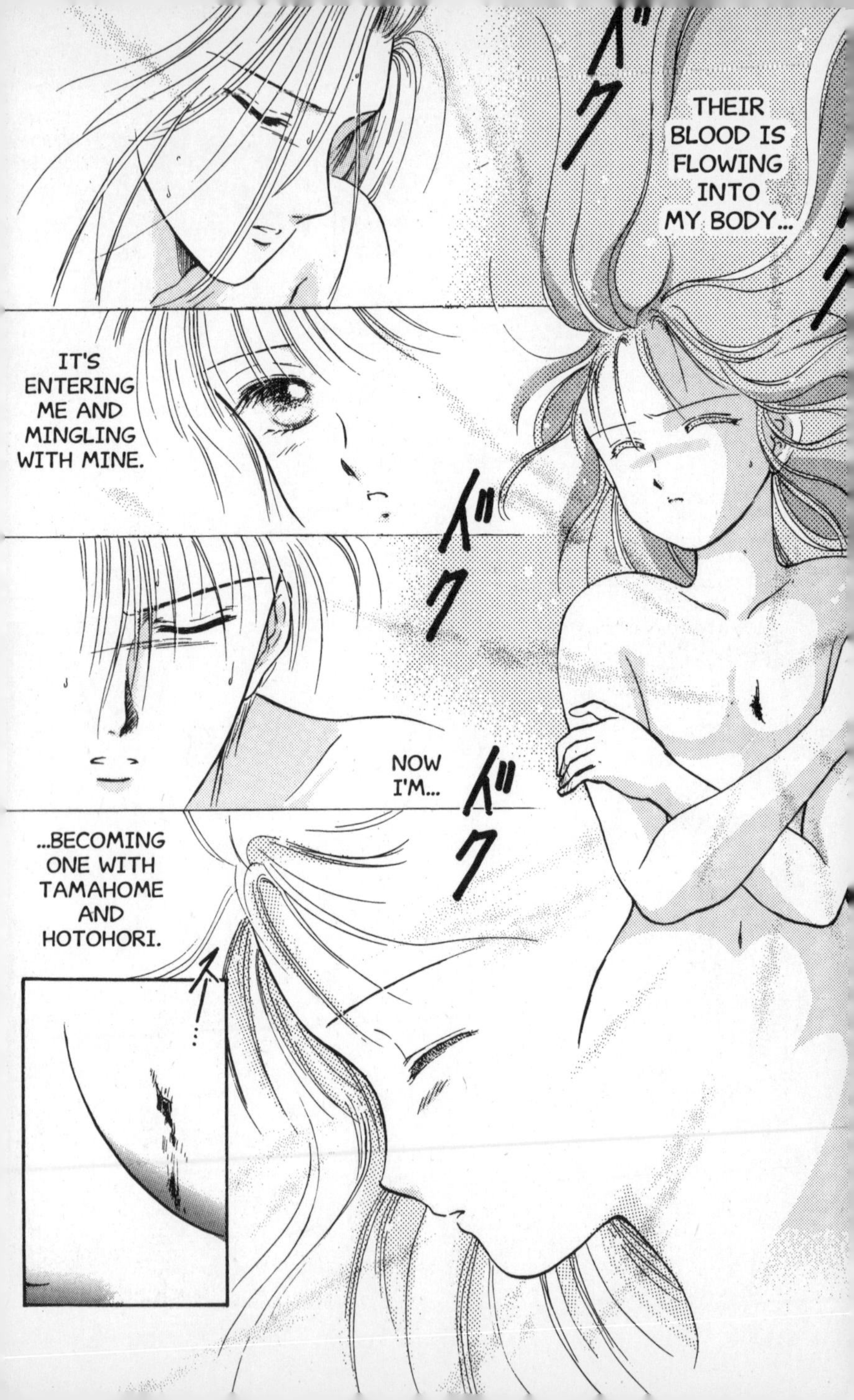
THEIR BLOOD IS FLOWING INTO MY BODY...
IT'S ENTERING ME AND MINGLING WITH MINE.
NOW I'M...
...BECOMING ONE WITH TAMAHOME AND HOTOHORI.

HERE IT IS! "THE LIVING BLOOD OF TAMAHOME AND HOTOHORI SUFFUSED THE BODY OF THE YOUNG LADY."
THIS IS WHERE YOU MUST BE, MIAKA!
THE PAIN'S GOING AWAY.
AND THE BLOOD... IT'S DISAP-PEARING!
THE POLICE !?
GAK!
CITY CENTRAL LIBRARY
SO THIS GIRL SUDDENLY STARTED BLEEDING, THEN SHE COLLAPS-ED?
THAT WAS HERE?
YES! RIGHT ON THOSE STAIRS!

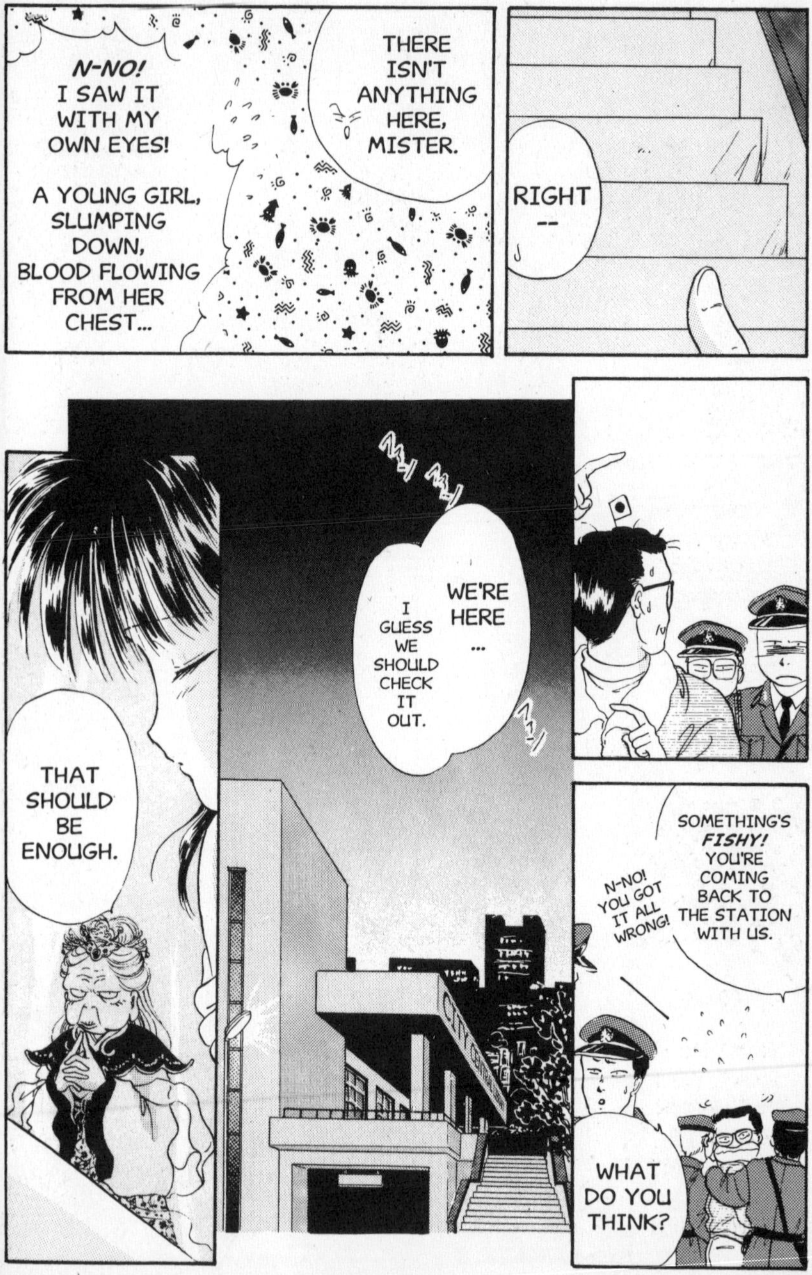
THERE ISN'T ANYTHING HERE, MISTER.
N-NO! I SAW IT WITH MY OWN EYES!
A YOUNG GIRL, SLUMPING DOWN, BLOOD FLOWING FROM HER CHEST...
RIGHT --
SOMETHING'S FISHY! YOU'RE COMING BACK TO THE STATION WITH US.
N-NO! YOU GOT IT ALL WRONG!
WHAT DO YOU THINK?
WE'RE HERE...
I GUESS WE SHOULD CHECK IT OUT.
THAT SHOULD BE ENOUGH.

PUT ON CLOTHES.
TH-- THANK YOU.
HUH!
TAMAHOME! HOTOHORI! ARE YOU OKAY!?
YEAH... I THINK SO.
THANK YOU! YOU'VE DONE SO MUCH FOR ME!
IF YOU ARE WELL, WE WISH NOTHING MORE.
NOW THAT MIAKA'S FEELING BETTER...
...I'LL TELL YOU HOW TO RETURN.
MIAKA!
REMEMBER THAT YOU OWE YOUR *LIFE* TO TAMAHOME AND HOTOHORI!

LISTEN CAREFULLY, MIAKA. YOU'VE STAYED IN THIS WORLD TOO LONG.
THEREFORE, YOU CANNOT RETURN SIMPLY BY FINDING AN OPENING, THE WAY YOU DID PREVIOUSLY.
HOWEVER, THERE ARE TWO THINGS THAT CONNECT YOU TO THE OTHER WORLD.
THE FIRST IS SOMETHING THAT IS "IDENTICAL HERE AS THERE." WE NEED SOMETHING THAT CAN REACH BOTH POINTS.
THAT'S SPEAKING METAPHORICALLY, OF COURSE!
SOMETHING THAT IS "IDENTICAL HERE AS THERE."
KINDA LIKE A RIDDLE.
ポン

OUR UNI-FORM !!
THAT'LL WORK!
THE SECOND IS A STRONG WILL AND DEEP, INTENSELY SHARED FEELINGS.
!!
IT MUST CONNECT WITH SOME-ONE WHO OWNS THE IDENTICAL THING.
OR WITH A PLACE THAT IS RELATED TO THIS THING.
RELATED...
SO THEN A PLACE LIKE MY SCHOOL, WHERE THEY WEAR THE SAME UNIFORM.
MIAKA!! I'M RIGHT HERE!
COME BACK HOME!

IF CIRCUMSTANCES WERE NORMAL AND ALL SEVEN CELESTIAL WARRIORS WERE PRESENT, THIS WOULD BE EASY.
BUT NURIKO IS THE ONLY UNWOUNDED WARRIOR...
...AND THE AMOUNT OF SPIRITUAL ENERGY NEEDED IS ENORMOUS.
YUI!
WE CAN DO IT.
YES. WE CAN RETURN HER TO HER HOME.
DON'T YOU WORRY ABOUT A THING, MIAKA.
I'M A GOOD GIRL THESE DAYS.

BUT IN RETURN, YOU'LL HAVE TO PROMISE TO COME BACK.
EVERY-BODY'LL BE WAITING FOR YOU.
THAT'S RIGHT.
I'M GOING BACK HOME...
THAT MEANS I WON'T BE ABLE TO SEE TAMA-HOME.
SHALL WE COMMENCE ...

CONCEN-TRATE YOUR ENERGY ON MIAKA.
MIAKA, PICTURE YOUR WORLD IN YOUR MIND...
...AND CONCENTRATE ON THE IMAGE.

TAMAHOME AND HOTOHORI ARE WOUNDED... SHOULD I REALLY BE GOING HOME?
I'M SORRY EVERY-BODY.
LOOK AT EVERY-THING I'VE PUT YOU THROUGH.
!!
YOU FOOL! CONCEN-TRATE!

C'MON, MIAKA! YOU CAN DO IT!
CONCENTRATE ON ME!
IF YOU DON'T, YOU COULD SPEND ETERNITY IN THE BREACH BETWEEN TIME AND SPACE!
OH-
-NO.
THIS IS THE POLICE!!
WHO'S THERE!? OPEN UP!

MIAKA!!
HURRY!!
I CAN'T!!
THE HARDER I TRY TO CONCENTRATE, THE MORE... I *CAN'T!*

YOU IDIOT! COME BACK HOME! COME HOME, DAMMIT!
YOUR MOM AND BROTHER ARE WORRIED SICK OVER YOU!
YOU AND ME! WE'VE BEEN TOGETHER FOR SO LONG!
YUI ...
EVER SINCE KINDERGARTEN!!
WE PROMISED EACH OTHER WE'D GO TO THE SAME HIGH SCHOOL, DIDN'T WE!?

I WANT US TO GO TO THE SAME HIGH SCHOOL ...
COME OUT OF THERE!
LOOKS LIKE WE'LL HAVE TO BREAK IT DOWN!
LET'S PASS OUR EXAMS TOGE-THER!

I CAN FEEL EVERY-BODY'S ENERGY.
THAT'S RIGHT. CALM DOWN, MIAKA.
YOU'RE GOING HOME ...
BACK TO MOM...
TO KEISUKE...
BACK TO MY FRIENDS...

BACK TO MY OWN WORLD.
MIAKA!
BACK HOME !!

CHAPTER ELEVEN
LONGING FOR YOU

I FEEL LIKE I'M BURNING UP!
JUST LIKE THE FIRST TIME I ENTERED "THE UNIVERSE OF FOUR GODS."
...I'M COMING HOME.
I'M FINALLY COMING *HOME* !!

パリパリ
パリパリ

パリパリ
バッ

GWEEN
OUCHIE!
THIS REALLY IS MY SCHOOL !!
SO I DID GET OUT OF THE BOOK!
AT THE TIME ...

AND YUI CALLED TO ME FROM OUTSIDE THE BOOK...
TAMAHOME, HOTOHORI AND NURIKO SHARED THEIR POWER WITH ME...
THANKS TO THEM, I MADE IT BACK *HOME.*
BUT SOME-THING'S WEIRD.
IF MY SCHOOL UNIFORM IS THE CONNECTION BETWEEN THIS WORLD AND THE WORLD OF THE BOOK...
もたくた
WHY DIDN'T I WIND UP WHERE YUI IS?

MIAKA !!
HAMAMURA
KEISUKE!!

YOU IDIOT!!
WHERE WERE YOU!?
EVERY-ONE WAS WORRIED *SICK* OVER YOU!!
I-- I'M SORRY.
SIGH
WELL, I'M GLAD I FOUND YOU.
GEEZ, I SPENT *TWO WHOLE HOURS* RUNNING AROUND!
HUH?
TWO HOURS !?
NO WAY!
ONLY TWO HOURS !?
Y'MEAN, IT'S STILL DECEMBER !?

しーん
I-- I THOUGHT IT HAD BEEN *MONTHS.*
BUT IT'S ONLY BEEN HOURS?
SO MOM'S STILL MAD!
I APOLOGIZE FOR HITTING YOU.
BUT THAT DOESN'T GIVE YOU THE RIGHT TO DISAPPEAR FOR HOURS.
LIKE I SAID ...
...I WAS STUCK INSIDE THE BOOK AT THE LIBRARY--
KER THUNK

YOU'RE GOING TO INSULT ME WITH THAT LIE AGAIN!?
DO YOU KNOW HOW WORRIED WE WERE ABOUT YOU?
C'MON, MOM. AT LEAST WE KNOW SHE'S ALL RIGHT.
LET ME GIVE HER A TALKING TO.
HERE...
...HAVE SOME HOT COCOA.
AND I'LL HAVE COFFEE.
SO LET'S SEE.
YOU WERE AT SCHOOL ALL ALONG, RIGHT?
NO! LIKE I SAID...

Oracle

Here's a little confession. I really like Miaka's older brother, Keisuke. If he existed, I might really fall for him. His younger classmates would fall for him -- he's so nice. He probably would have been the captain of whatever team he was on. If both he and his friend had a crush on the same girl, he would pair the girl up with his friend. He's really fond of his sister (not like she's his pet or anything). My assistant, S., on the other hand, is part of the "Tamahome" faction. I gotta say... Yeah, I like Tamahome too, as a manga character. I guess Tamahome's the most popular amongst you readers. I heard that one of the reasons for his popularity is that he resembles Manato in "Prepubescence." S. was totally mortified by this comment, insisting that they had totally different personalities. I suppose Tamahome wouldn't exactly be thrilled to find he was popular because he looked like someone else. Asuka and Miaka are both my main characters and so have the same look, but their personalities are totally different. (But do they look so much alike? Well, maybe they do, but should every manga artist have to draw a different face for every new protagonist?)

I think that Tamahome is more mature than Manato. Manato's an ordinary urban high-school boy. He **does** have his lighter side, though. Tamahome, on the other hand, had to work hard and mature, so he's more in control of his feelings. He might seem a little insensitive (e.g. when Nuriko says something outrageous), but that's not his true self at all. In fact, he might be more sensitive than Hotohori. He has some powerful emotions kept inside. I've never written a character like him before. Tamahome is really strong, but he might have some profound weaknesses. He seems really upbeat, when in fact he has a dark side. He can be emotional and yet be cool. He has a child-like face yet he can be so mature. So S. and I think that he is full of contradictory traits...

So that's what he's like!

HMM...
SO LET ME GET THIS STRAIGHT. YOU WERE AT THE LIBRARY AND GOT SUCKED INTO A BOOK CALLED "THE UNIVERSE OF THE FOUR GODS?"
AND IF YOU FIND ALL SEVEN PEOPLE WHO MAKE UP THESE "CONSTELLATIONS OF SUZAKU," THEN THIS GOD "SUZAKU" APPEARS AND GRANTS YOU A WISH?
AND BECAUSE YOU WANTED TO PASS YOUR ENTRANCE EXAMS, YOU ACCEPTED YOUR ROLE AS THIS "PRIESTESS OF SUZAKU?"
こく
こく
こく
THEN HOTOHORI, EMPEROR OF THE HONG-NAN EMPIRE, ASKED ME TO PROTECT HIS COUNTRY!
HE'S ABSOLUTELY GORGEOUS, BY THE WAY.
WE WENT TO TAI YI-JUN SO THAT I COULD RETURN HOME...
FEVER!?!
YOU DON'T BELIEVE ME! BUT THANKS TO YUI, I MADE IT BACK SO...
OKAY, OKAY.

LET'S JUST SAY YOUR ACCOUNT'S TRUE...
...THAT BOOK IS PRETTY DANGER-OUS!
THE STORY MUST BE SOME KIND OF CURSE.
IF YOU TRANSLATE THE SUTRAS, THERE'S A CONTINUING STORY THERE, TOO.
IT DOESN'T SEEM LIKE YOUR BOOK IS A SUTRA. MUST BE SOME VARIETY OF MAGIC TOME.
I KNOW THAT GIRLS LIKE TO READ BOOKS WITH MYSTICAL CHARMS.
THE OLDER THE SPELL IS, THE MORE POWERFUL IT CAN BE. SO MANY OF THEM ARE DANGER-OUS.
DANGEROUS?
THERE'S ALWAYS A SACRIFICE THAT GOES WITH A WISH!

IN THE EXTREME CASES, WHEN PRACTITIONERS OF BLACK MAGIC IN THE WEST WANTED THEIR WISHES GRANTED,
THEY'D SACRIFICE A *WOMAN!* WOO! IT'S SO *SCARY!!*
KEISUKE! I'M SCARED OF YOUR *FACE*!
OWHA TAFOO LIAM
YOU MAY *SAY* THAT, BUT YOU DON'T BELIEVE IN ANY OF THIS
AND TAMA-HOME ISN'T DANGER-OUS!
MIAKA, DO YOU UNDERSTAND YOUR *OWN* POSITION?
YOUR EXAMS ARE COMING UP. I KNOW YOU'RE UNDER A LOT OF PRESSURE, BUT TRY NOT TO UPSET MOM, HUH?
I'M JUST WORRIED ABOUT YOU.

WHETHER YOU'RE TELLING THE TRUTH OR NOT, *DON'T* GO NEAR THAT BOOK AGAIN!
JUST FORGET YOU SAW IT!
トゥルルル…
トゥルルル…
I WONDER WHERE YUI IS.
IS SHE ASLEEP ALREADY?
I GUESS I'LL SEE HER AT SCHOOL TOMORROW.
パタン
AND HERE I'M FINALLY BACK...

キイ…
I FEEL KINDA LONELY.
HOTOHORI
カリ…
TAMAHOME
NURIKO
TAMAHOME
YOU'LL HAVE TO *PROMISE* TO COME BACK.
THERE'S NO DANGER, RIGHT? TAMAHOME...
HOW COULD I "FORGET I SAW IT?"

ONE THING'S FOR SURE THOUGH...
HERE, I'M NOT THE PRIESTESS OF SUZAKU. ALL I AM IS...
...AN ORDINARY STUDENT STUDYING FOR MY EXAMS.
GOOD MORN-ING.
MORNING. HEY, DID YOU WATCH--
すたたたたた
FU! MORIN!!
HUH?

RUBBARUBBARUBBARUBBA
LONG TIME NO *SEE!* HOW HAVE YOU BEEN?
STOP IT! STOP IT! STOP IT!
WHAT'S GOTTEN INTO YOU, MIAKA!?
WE JUST SAW EACH OTHER *YESTERDAY!*
BUT I MISSED YOU SO MUCH!! HAVE A *KISS!*
SMAK
EVEN MY SMELLY SHOE BOX SEEMS LIKE IT'S CHANEL NO. 5!
STILL STINKS, THO—
IS SHE LOSING IT?
LOOKS LIKE IT.
TIME TO TAKE ATTENDANCE.
I'M HERE! MIAKA YŪKI! RIGHT HERE!
WAIT TILL YOU'RE CALLED.
NEXT... HONGO!

YUI HONGO.
THAT'S ODD. SHE HARDLY EVER MISSES CLASS.
NEXT, MIYOSHI!
HERE.
YUI'S OUT?
THAT'S WEIRD. SHE SOUNDED SO ENERGETIC WHEN SHE CALLED FROM OUTSIDE THE BOOK.
SHE DIDN'T ANSWER THE PHONE.
I WONDER WHAT HAPPENED.
ALL RIGHT, TAKE OUT YOUR PENCILS AND PUT EVERYTHING ELSE AWAY.

WE'VE GOT A POP QUIZ.
YER KIDDING!
STOP YOUR GRIPING! IF YOU'VE BEEN STUDYING FOR YOUR ENTRANCE EXAMS, THEN THIS'LL BE A CINCH.
MIAKA, PUT YOUR TEXTBOOK AWAY! IT'S A POP QUIZ!
I HATE POP QUIZZES!
A-- A POP TART?
Q-U-I-Z!
KLUNK
BEGIN!
ARGH-
-THIS IS THE WORST.
I WONDER WHAT HAPPENED TO YUI.
LET'S SEE.

...
I--
I'LL JUST SKIP THIS FIRST QUESTION.
NEXT...
...
...
A BREEZE.

カリ
カリ
チッ チッ
ガク
ガク
ガク
カリ
カリ
カリ
カリ
WH-- WHAT AM I GONNA DO?
EVERYONE ELSE IS DOING *FINE*.

HOW MANY MONTHS DID I SPEND INSIDE THE BOOK WITHOUT STUDYING?
カクカクカク
YUI...
TAMA-HOME...
ポキン
WHAT IF THIS WERE THE REAL ENTRANCE EXAMS!?
TAMA-HOME...
I'D FAIL FOR SURE!
チッチッ
カリ
HELP ME, *TAMA-HOME!!*
DON'T WORRY, MIAKA.

YOU'LL BE JUST FINE.
IT'S JUST THE SUDDEN SHOCK.
I'LL BE RIGHT BEHIND YOU.

TAMA-
HOME!!
WHAT'S
YOUR
PROBLEM
YŪKI!?
TAMA-
HOME?
WHERE
ARE
YOU?

ガタッ
TAMA-HOME!?
YŪKI!?
TAMA-HOME!
WHERE ARE YOU?
WHERE DID YOU GO?

TAMA-
HOME!
ズルッ
HE
ISNT...
...HERE.

HE ISN'T...
HE ISN'T ANYWHERE IN THE WORLD!
TAMA-HOME...

NO MATTER HOW MUCH I *MISS* YOU...
SOB
"*DON'T* GO NEAR THAT BOOK AGAIN."
"FORGET YOU SAW IT!"
YOU EXIST *ONLY* IN THAT BOOK.
I'M SORRY, KEISUKE.
I NEED TO...

I GOTTA SEE *TAMA-HOME*!!
OH!
BUT FIRST I HAVE TO TALK TO YUI!
I NEED TO THANK HER!
ガチャ
はあ はあ
WE *HAVE* TO CALL THE POLICE!
EXCUSE ME...
MIAKA!
WHERE-- WHERE'S YUI!?

WE BOTH GOT BACK FROM OUR BUSINESS TRIPS THIS MORNING, AND SHE'S *GONE!*
HUH
WE FOUND THIS NOTE.
I'm out to search for Miaka I'll be back as soon as I find her.
Yui
SHE'S ALWAYS BEEN A GOOD CHILD! SHE WOULD *NEVER* STAY OUT ALL NIGHT!
SHE WENT LOOKING FOR *YOU!* I *DEMAND* AN EXPLANATION!
YUI'S MISSING!?
WHERE'S MY DAUGHTER!?

PARDON THE PARODY

WHY IT ALWAYS OUT OF CHAPTER 9?

BY
Y.W.
(MANGA ARTIST)

CHAPTER TWELVE
REACHING OUT

MIAKA! I WANT TO KNOW WHERE YUI IS!
CALM DOWN. IT'S NOT HER FAULT!
YUI'S *MISSING!?* WHAT'S GOING ON?
LET'S LOOK AROUND, *THEN* WE'LL CONTACT THE POLICE.
SHE WAS AT THE LIBRARY. WAS SHE IN THAT PRIVATE ROOM?
SHE HAD "THE UNI-VERSE OF THE FOUR GODS" OPEN.
SHE *COULDN'T* HAVE...
SHE COULDN'T HAVE....
四神天地書

I-- I'LL HELP LOOK, TOO!
YUI!
バターン
HMM?
HUH? IS THAT YOU, MOM?
ガタガタン

SO NOW YOU'RE A PETTY THIEF!? WHAT ABOUT *SCHOOL?*
YOU'RE SUPPOSED TO BE IN COLLEGE!
SWEETS GALORE
I DON'T HAVE ANY CLASSES TODAY! *HEY!*
バタバタ
YOU *RUNNING AWAY* FROM HOME!?
I HAVE TO GO FIND YUI!!

THIS ISN'T *JUST* ABOUT FINDING HER!
I DON'T THINK I'LL BE ABLE TO ESCAPE THE BOOK UNTIL I REACH THE VERY LAST PAGE.
SHE'S BEEN SUCKED INTO "THE UNIVERSE OF THE FOUR GODS!"
THAT *HAS* TO BE IT! THE FIRST TIME, WE WERE BOTH SUCKED IN!
I *HAVE* TO HELP HER.
KEISUKE...
THAT BOOK AGAIN!? I TOLD YOU TO FORGET ALL ABOUT THAT BOOK!

FROM THE MOMENT I OPENED THE "THE UNIVERSE OF THE FOUR GODS"...THE MOMENT I MET TAMAHOME...
I'M SORRY!!
COME BACK HERE, MIAKA!
CITY CENTRAL LIBRA
DID YOU HEAR ABOUT LAST NIGHT?
THE POLICE CAME ABOUT SOME GIRL WHO WAS BLEEDING.
WHISPER WHISPER WHISPER
THAT'S NOT ALL.
THEY HEARD A GIRL'S VOICE COMING FROM THAT RESTRICTED ROOM, BUT NOBODY WAS THERE.
WOW! THAT'S TOO WEIRD.

RESTRICTED PRIVATE LIBRARY
KEEP OUT
カチャ
FIXING THE LOCK
とたとたとた
HM?
THWKAM
SORRY!
MAIKA!!
BLOCK THE DOOR, KEISUKE! DON'T LET ANYBODY IN!
ドドッ
FOUR GODS... FOUR GODS... HERE IT IS!

I'M COMING, YUI...
...TAMA-HOME!
しゅるっ
H-HUH?
OH, YEAH.
KEISUKE... KEEP THIS AND DON'T *EVER* LOSE IT! IT'S THE CONNECTION THAT WILL KEEP US IN CONTACT!
PLEASE TELL MOM THAT I'M SORRY.
I'M GOING.

"GOING?" WHAT DO YOU *MEAN!?*

NO WAY !!
NO--
CITY CENTRAL LIB
WHAT ARE THEY THINKING?
THE SITUATION SHOULD NEVER HAVE BECOME THIS GRAVE!

While Asuka has suffered through many hard times, the only hardship for Miaka is studying for the entrance exams (which are pretty hard, to be sure). She has a nice brother; she's carefree and childish. That's why she'll never have the same mature quality Asuka has. I was wondering why this was, only to realize that they had different upbringings, so their personalities would have to differ. I surprised myself. My protagonists are all the same in their energy and positive outlook. But in terms of her naiveté, Miaka is just an average junior-high-school girl. Unlike Asuka, who soon finds happiness, Miaka's life is going to get worse and worse. She might mature like Asuka as the story comes to a close. But the pain makes them grow, and growth is something I enjoy seeing. It's interesting to see how these characters grow up on their own. It isn't one of the things I plan. By the way, my friends have started to like either Hotohori or Nuriko. Putting Hotohori aside for a moment... They all hated Nuriko when she (he) kissed Tamahome. Later, they started warming up to him, but once they found out he was gay, they disliked him again. Now that's a busy character! Recently, I'm glad to say that I've been hearing from more and more people who like him. I like him a lot! Children who read about cross-dressers don't like them, but readers who've graduated middle school seem to like that type of character a lot. This story is going to be really long so I'll do my best to make it through to the end. Stick with me, okay? The situation has been pretty hard up to this point, but this was the easy part! Miaka and Tamahome are really going to suffer. But however much they suffer, it's going to be twice as hard on me! You see, I'm just too nice and sweet a person. Ten demerits to anyone who just threw this book on the floor and stomped on it.

To be continued in the next issue!!

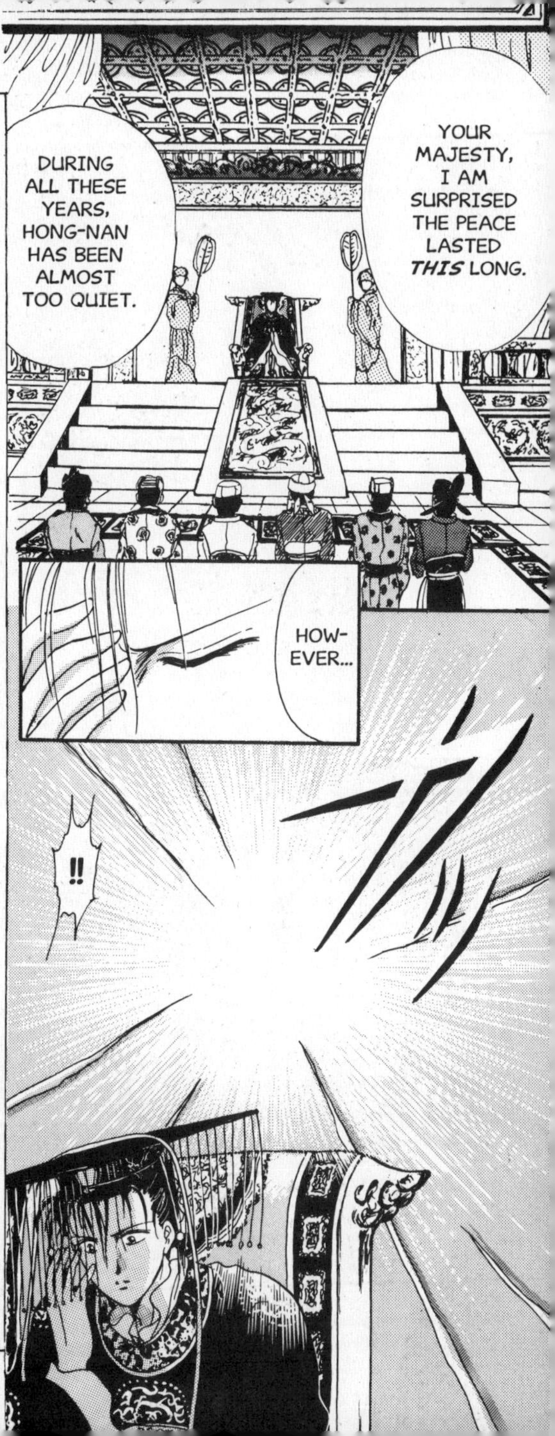

バリバリ…
どす…
OOPS?
WOAAAH
YOUR MAJESTY!
...
HA HA HAAA...
SORRY, HOTOHORI.
!!
THE PRIESTESS OF SUZAKU!!
WHAT?!
SHE'S BACK!
Yessir Yessir
HA HA HAAA
MIAKA YŪKI REPORTING FOR DUTY!

I--
HOW I *MISSED* YOU, MIAKA!
HOTOHORI.
HE *REALLY* MISSED ME!
WHAT!? THREE MONTHS HAVE ALREADY PASSED SINCE I LEFT!?
THERE'S BEEN SOME TROUBLE IN THE INTERVAL.
I MUST ASK YOU, THE PRIESTESS OF SUZAKU, FOR A FAVOR.

YOU *MUST* FIND THE OTHER FOUR CONSTELLATIONS OF SUZAKU AS SOON AS POSSIBLE.
RELATIONS WITH OUR NEIGHBORING COUNTRY QU-DONG HAVE DETERIORATED.
EVERY YEAR WE SEND AMBASSADORS WITH PEACE TREATIES.
WHAT DO YOU MEAN?
YOU MAY CONSIDER REMOVING YOUR BACKPACK.
RADDA RADDA
OUR AMBASSADORS HAVE NOT RETURNED! IN FACT, QU-DONG ACCUSES US OF HAVING NEVER SENT THEM IN THE FIRST PLACE.
NOW ISN'T THAT ODD?
THEIR MINISTERS WERE OUTRAGED, AND THEY DECLARED WAR. THEY'VE SOUGHT OUR LANDS SINCE ANTIQUITY.
W-- WAR...

HOTOHORI! DID YOU SEE YUI!? A GIRL DRESSED LIKE ME, BUT WITH SHORT HAIR?
I HAVEN'T...
IF THERE'S A WAR, YUI COULD GET CAUGHT IN THE CROSSFIRE!
YUI!
THEN... WHERE...
MIAKA... HONG-NAN IS NOT A STRONG COUNTRY. GATHER THE SEVEN CONSTELLA-TIONS OF SUZAKU *QUICKLY!*
PLEASE!?!

"THE POWER OF THE SUZAKU"
たたたっ
THAT'S RIGHT! ONCE I GATHER THE SEVEN CONSTELLATIONS OF THE SUZAKU, MY WISH WILL COME TRUE.
I CAN FIND YUI THAT WAY!
I'LL FIND TAMAHOME, AND WE'LL SEARCH TOGETHER...
MIAKA!
I THOUGHT IT WAS YOU!
NURIKO!
I'M LOOKING FOR TAMAHOME.
...

HE'S NOT HERE.
HE MADE SOME MONEY, SO HE WAS HEADING HOME. THAT WAS A FEW DAYS BACK.
I SEE...
HE WASN'T WAITING FOR ME AFTER ALL...
......
ALL RIGHT THEN!
YOU'RE GOING TO SEARCH FOR TAMA-HOME?
ON YOUR OWN?
NO, NURIKO'S COMING WITH ME!
RIGHT !?!

HE'S EVEN DRESSED AS A GUY!
IT'S JUST HARDER TO PRO- TECT YOU IN WOMEN'S CLOTHES.
AND LOOKIN' GOOD, TOO!
RUB RUB
.....
FEELING A LITTLE ILL.
VERY WELL... BUT DO BE CAREFUL.
THERE ARE REPORTS OF QU-DONG SPIES IN THE AREA...
HOW COULD TAMAHOME BE THINKING OF *MONEY* AT A TIME LIKE THIS?

MMMBL MMMBL
I CAN'T BELIEVE YOU CAME BACK. TAMA-BABY WILL BE SO HAPPY TO SEE YOU.
DID YOU FORGET ABOUT ME?
IT'S BEEN THREE LONG MONTHS...
THE TRUTH IS, I WANTED TO BE ENCIRCLED BY YOUR ARMS THE MOMENT I RETURNED.
EVER SINCE YOU'VE BEEN AWAY, HE'S BEEN OUT OF IT.
YOU SHOULD'VE SEEN HIM.
DUH
THAT'S A PLATE, DUMMY.
CHOMP CHOMP
DUHHH
BUT THERE'S NO NEED TO WORRY.

TAMAHOME'S STUCK ON YOU.
THAT'S NOT TRUE. HE *TOLD* ME HE DIDN'T HAVE ANY FEELINGS FOR ME.
HE PROBABLY JUST WASN'T AWARE OF IT.
...HM?
HEY, HOW'D IT GET SO DARK!?
NOW THAT'S WEIRD! MAYBE WE TOOK THE WRONG PATH.

OUCHIE!
HEY... ARE YOU ALL RIGHT?
OH!
MY RIBBON'S GONE!!
W- WHERE IS IT!?
I'LL LOSE MY CONNECTION TO KEISUKE WITHOUT MY RIBBON.
HM...
HERE IT IS.

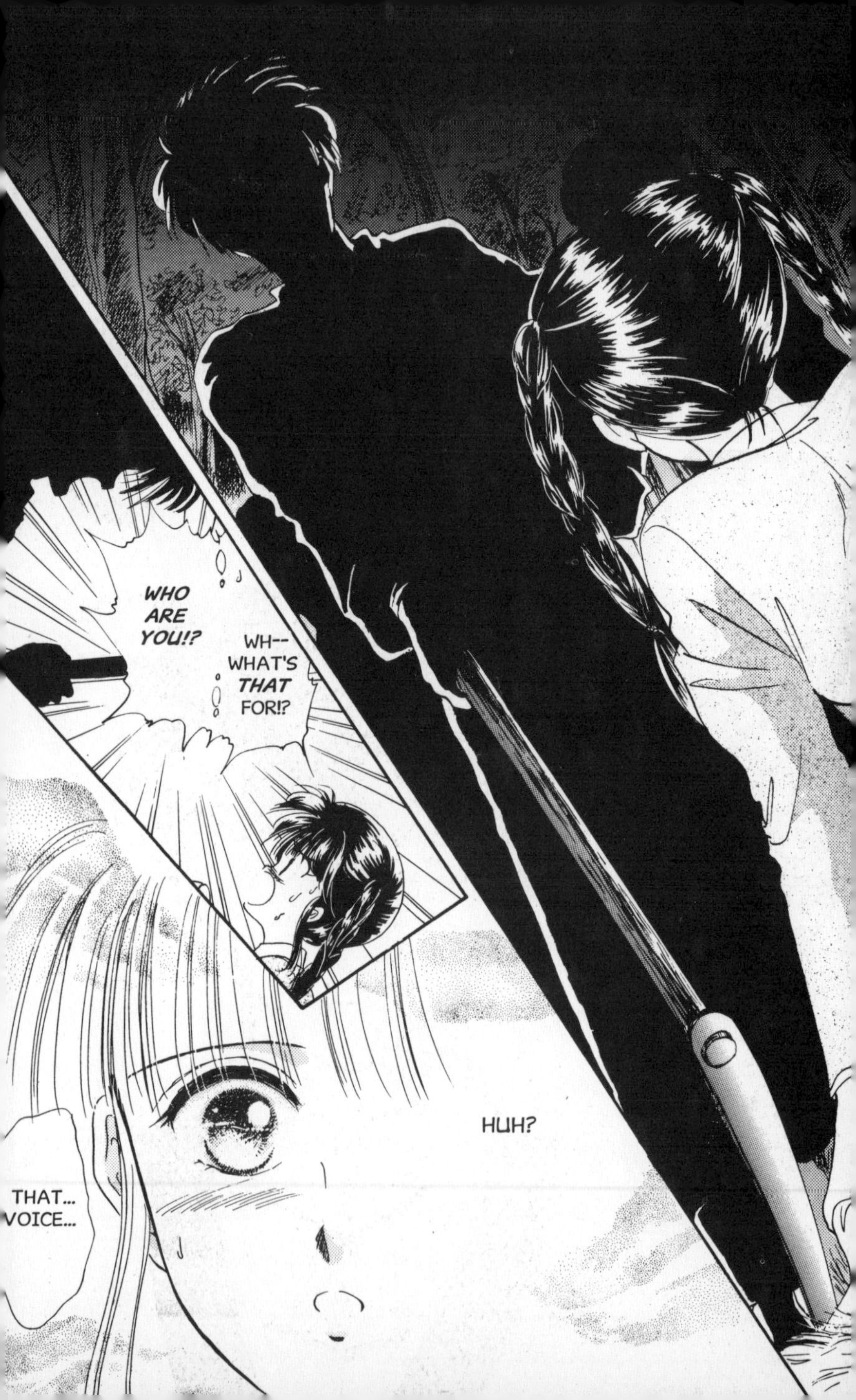
WH-- WHAT'S THAT FOR!?
WHO ARE YOU!?
HUH?
THAT... VOICE...

たったっ
MIAKA?

TAMA-HOME...
CAN IT... IS IT *REALLY* YOU?
MIAKA.
HAS IT ONLY BEEN THREE MONTHS?
I SWEAR IT FEELS LIKE A THOUSAND YEARS.

TAMAHOME!

…トクン
トクン
I MISSED YOU!
トクン
HE'S SO WARM...
I CAN FEEL THE EATING OF HIS HEART...
トクン
I DON'T CARE IF HE IS FROM ANOTHER WORLD...
...AS LONG AS WE CAN BE TOGETHER.

I CAN'T HELP IT!
THERE'S NO ONE I LOVE AS MUCH AS HIM!
YOU LOOK WELL. DID YOU SEE YOUR MOM?
UH-HUH. WE DIDN'T EXACTLY REACH A TRUCE THOUGH.
HEY, ARE YOU GUYS AWARE YOU HAVE AN *AUDIENCE!?*
はっ
じ ——
TAMAHOME, WHO ARE THESE PEOPLE?

ざわっ
OH... THIS IS MIAKA, THE PRIESTESS OF SUZAKU.
AND THIS GUY'S QUEER.
KLUNK
I-- I MEAN... THIS GUY'S NURIKO, A CONSTELLATION OF SUZAKU LIKE ME.
YOU HEARD ABOUT QU-DONG, RIGHT? SUSPICIOUS FOLKS ARE CROPPIN' UP LATELY.
AND GUARD DUTY DOESN'T PAY TOO BAD.
AS LONG AS I'M AROUND, THE VILLAGE'LL BE SAFE!
TAMAHOME... YOU HAVEN'T CHANGED. I'M SO GLAD YOU'RE WITH ME.
AAUGH-- OUR TORCHES HAVE GONE OUT! BUT THERE'S NO WIND!
WHAT'S GOING ON?
I DON'T GET IT!

TO BE CONTINUED IN VOLUME 3:DISCIPLE

ABOUT THE AUTHOR

Yû Watase was born on March 5 in a town near Osaka, Japan, and she was raised there before moving to Tokyo to follow her dream of creating manga. In the decade since her debut short story, *Pajama de Ojama* ("An Intrusion in Pajamas"), she has produced more than 50 compiled volumes of short stories and continuing series. Her latest series, *Zettai Kareshi* ("He'll Be My Boyfriend"), is currently running in the anthology magazine *Shôjo Comic*. Watase's long-running horror/romance story *Ceres: Celestial Legend* and her most recent completed series, *Alice 19th*, are now available in North America published by VIZ. She loves science fiction, fantasy and comedy.

The Fushigi Yûgi Guide to Sound Effects

Most of the sound effects in FUSHIGI YÛGI are the way Yû Watase created them, in their original Japanese.

We created this glossary for a page-by-page, panel-by-panel explanation of the action and background noises. By using this guide, you may even learn some Japanese.

The glossary lists page and panel number. For example, page 1, panel 3, would be listed as 1.3.

27.1 FX: Su (headache suddenly lifting)
27.3 FX: Chapo (splorsh)
27.4 FX: Buku buku (glug glug)

28.3 FX: Basha basha (splash splash)
28.4 FX: Suuuuu (swooosh)
28.5 FX: Basha basha (splash splash)

29.1 FX: Zazaaaa (splorsh)
FX: Za (crunch)
29.3 FX: Shu (whoosh)

30.1 FX: Doboom (sploosh)
30.2 FX: Buku buku (glug glug)
30.3 FX: Shiiiin (silence)

31.3 FX: Pon (thump)
31.5 FX: Hata (gasp)

32.2 FX: Shiiiiin (wind blowing)
32.3 FX: Doki doki doki doki doki doki doki (ba-dump ba-dump ba-dump ba-dump ba-dump ba-dump ba-dump)

33.3 FX: Zaba (sploosh)

35.3 FX: Bata bata (struggle struggle)
35.5 FX: Pala (slip)

36.3 FX: Shiiiin (silence)

37.4 FX: Ku ku (snicker snicker)

CHAPTER EIGHT: A DARK INVITATION

43.5 FX: Pii chi chi chi (tweet chirp chirp chirp)

44.2 FX: Basa basa (flap flap)
44.5 FX: Doki (ba-dump)

CHAPTER SEVEN: THE AIMLESS HEART

9.1 FX: Ha ha ha ha (huff huff huff huff)

11.3 FX: Gyu (clench)
11.4 FX: Su (swoosh)

13.3 FX: Ha (gasp)

15.4 FX: Doki (ba-dump)

16.2 FX: Dokun dokun dokun (ba-dump ba-dump ba-dump)

17.5 FX: Bishi (vwip)

18.2 FX: Dota bata (hustle scramble)
FX: Sawa sawa (fluster fluster)

19.2 FX: Doki (ba-dump)
19.5 FX: Pui (twirl)
19.6 FX: Giii (creak)

20.1 FX: Ka (clop)

21.2 FX: Kapo kapo (clop clop)
21.4 FX: Kapo kapo kapo (clop clop clop)

22.2 FX: Gaaa (snore)
22.4 FX: Haa haa (huff huff)

23.5 FX: Sukaaa (snore)

24.1 FX: Gashi (clench)

25.3 FX: Buku (glug)
25.5 FX: Kula (dizzy)

26.4 FX: Ha ha (huff huff)
26.5 FX: Pasa (slipping out of clothes)

65.5 FX: Gaku (thump)
FX: Zulu (slump)

67.2 FX: Ba (swoosh)
67.3 FX: Palin (shatter)
67.4 FX: Dosu (stab)

68.2 FX: Gyaaahh (screech)
68.5 FX: Ba (fwoosh)
68.6 FX: Ssssssssskeeech (screech)
FX: Don (smack)

CHAPTER NINE: AWAKENING MEMORIES

70.3 FX: Gan (boot)
70.5 FX: Piku (ping)

71.1 FX: Ba (blood soaking through)
71.3 FX: Ba (goosh)
71.4 FX: Zulu (slump)
71.5 FX: Chalin (clank)

72.1 FX: Zubu (stab)
72.3 FX: Geho (cough)

73.2 FX: Gyaaahh (screech)
73.5 FX: Ba (fwoosh)

74.1 FX: Pan (tump)
74.2 FX: Don (thwack)
74.3-.4 FX: Ba (vwoosh)

75.1-.2 FX: Za (slash)
75.3 FX: Shu (swoosh)
75.4 FX: Zan (slice)
FX: Suto (tump)
75.5 FX: Gebo (cough)

77.4 FX: Suuuu (appearing out of thin air)

80.2 FX: Bi (rip)

85.4 FX: Ha ha ha ha (huff huff huff huff)

86.4 FX: Ba (fwoosh)
86.6 FX: Zulu zulu (drag drag)

87.1 FX: Zulu (drag)

88.1 FX: Zulu (drag)

45.1 FX: Doki doki doki doki (ba-dump ba-dump ba-dump ba-dump)

46.3 FX: Fu (float)
46.4 FX: Kulu kulu kulu kulu (whirl whirl whirl whirl)
46.5 FX: Fu (mirror disappearing)

47.1 FX: Kappo kappo (clop clop)
47.2 FX: Tsun (trip)
47.4 FX: Ba (whoosh)

48.2 FX: Da (dashing off)
FX: Dala dala (drip drip)
48.4 FX: Saaa (disappearing into the fog)

49.3 FX: Kon (kick)
49.4 FX: Kolo kolo kolo (roll roll roll)

51.1 FX: Supon (slipping through barrier)
51.3 FX: Don don (bam bam)
51.4 FX: Za (step)

53.2 FX: Gusha (stomp)
53.4 FX: Don don (bang bang)
53.5 FX: Nuli (shup)

54.2 FX: Don don (bang bang)

55.4 FX: Puha (gulp)
55.5 FX: Za (step)

56.1 FX: Doki (ba-dump)
56.3 FX: Dodododon (Ba-ba-bam)

58.4 FX: Don (thud)

60.5 FX: Da (dash)

61.1 FX: Suto (tump)
61.2 FX: Tata (run)
61.3 FX: Pa (flash)
61.6 FX: Chaki (drawing sword)

62.4 FX: Za (zhoosh)

64.2 FX: Sa (fwoosh)
64.3 FX: Ka (flash)
64.4 FX: Bali bali (zap zap)

115.2 FX: Kise kise (putting on clothes)

116.5 FX: Pon (clap)

121.4 FX: Buon (vwoosh)

122.3 FX: Don don don (bang bang bang)
122.4-.5 FX: Don don (bang bang)
122.5 FX: Don (bang)

127.1 FX: Ban (bam)
127.3 FX: Kaaaaaaaa (flash)

CHAPTER ELEVEN: LONGING FOR YOU

130.2 FX: Kaaaaaaaa (flash)

131.4 FX: Ka (flash)
131.5 FX: Pali pali pali pali
(crackle crackle crackle crackle)

132.1 FX: Pali pali (crackle crackle)
132.3 FX: Ba (gasp)

134.7 FX: Mota kuta (struggle struggle)

135.1 FX: Dota (thud)

137.3 FX: Shiiin (silence)

138.4 FX: Fuu fuu (blow blow)

140.1 FX: Koku koku koku (nod nod nod)

141.1 FX: Ki (creak)

143.2 FX: Tolulu (ring)
FX: Tolululu (ring)
143.5 FX: Patan (flop)

144.1 FX: Ki (creak)
144.2 FX: Kali (skritch)

145.2 FX: Suu (snore)
145.5 FX: Sutatatata (tump tump tump tump)

146.3 FX: Kun kun (sniff sniff)
146.4 FX: Zawa Zawa (chatter chatter)

147.5 FX: Pan pan (clap clap)

89.1 FX: Zulu (drag)
89.4 FX: Po (plip)

90.3 FX: Cha (chink)
90.4 FX: Ba (clutch)

92.1 FX: Zashu (slash)
FX: Bota bota (spatter spatter)
92.3 FX: Pikun (twitch)

97.1 FX: Suu (float)

98. 3 FX: Cha (chink)
98.4 FX: Ba (clutch)
98.5 FX: Grunch (grab)

CHAPTER TEN: COME BACK HOME

101.5 FX: Fuwa (float)

103.4 FX: Pala (flip)

104.1 FX: Pala (flip)

106.3 FX: Pou (glow)
106.4 FX: Suto (tump)
106.5 FX: Wala wala (shuffle shuffle)

107.4 FX: Baba (strip)
107.5 FX: Nuuu (wah)

109.4 FX: Pou (pong)

110.1 FX: Fuwa (float)
110.4-5 FX: Ba (vwip)

111.2 FX: Dokun (ba-dump)
111.3 FX: Doku doku (ba-dump ba-dump)

112.1-4 FX: Doku doku doku doku (ba-dump
ba-dump ba-dump ba-dump)
112.5 FX: Suuu (wound disappearing)

113.3 FX: Fan fan (sound of sirens)
113.4 FX: Fan fan fan (sound of sirens)
FX: Ki (screech)

114.5 FX: Fan fan fan (sound of sirens)

115.1 FX: Shu (bubble disappearing)
FX: Gakun (thud)

168.3 FX: Shulu (slip)
168.5 FX: Pala (flip)

169.2 FX: Ka (flash)

170.1 FX: Fu (disappearing)
FX: Tosa (thonk)

171.3 FX: Ka (flash)

172.1 FX: Dosu (thud)
172.2 FX: Beli beli (zzzt zzzt)

173.1 FX: Dokin (ba-dump)
173.3 FX: Doki doki doki (ba-dump ba-dump ba-dump)

176.1 FX: Ta ta (tump tump)

180.2 FX: Ka ka ka (clop clop clop)
180.3 FX: Hihiiiin (neigh)
180.4 FX: Ga (trip)

181.1 FX: Dotaaa (thud)
FX: Hihiiin (neigh)
181.3 FX: Hihiiin (neigh)
181.5 FX: Za (slice)

183.1 FX: Ta ta (tump tump)
183.2 FX: Fu (fwoo)

184.1 FX: Yoro (wobble)

186.1 FX: Tokun tokun tokun tokun (ba-dump ba-dump ba-dump ba-dump)

187.4 FX: Jiiii (stare)
FX: Ha (gasp)

188.1 FX: Zawa (murmur)
188.4 FX: Zawa zawa (chatter chatter)

189.2 FX: Su (shwoo)
189.4 FX: Su (shwooosh)

149.2 FX. Kali kali kali (skritch skritch skritch)
149.4 FX: Kali kali kali kali kali (skritch skritch skritch skritch skritch)
149.6 FX: Goshi goshi (erase erase)

150.1 FX: Gaku gaku gaku (tremble tremble tremble)
150.2 FX: Kali kali kali (skritch skritch skritch)
150.3 FX: Chi chi (tick tick)
150.4 FX: Kali kali kali (skritch skritch skritch)

151.1 FX: Kaku kaku kaku (tremble tremble tremble)
151.2 FX: Pokin (snap)
151.3 FX: Chi chi (tick tick)
151.4 FX: Kali kali kali kali kali kali kali (skritch skritch skritch skritch skritch skritch skritch)

154.1 FX: Gatan (kachunk)

155.2 FX: Zulu (slip)
155.3 FX: Dota (whud)

156.1 FX: Hikku (sniffle)

157.3 FX: Gyu (clench)
157.4 FX: Kachi kiiin kooon (tick bong bong)
157.5 FX: Kaan kooon kiin koon (bong bong bong bong)

158.4 FX: Ha ha (huff huff)
FX: Gacha (kachak)

160.3 FX: Za (slash)

CHAPTER TWELVE: REACHING OUT

163.3 FX: Batan (slam)
163.4 FX: Gata gatan (clank clatter)

164.2 FX: Bata bata (tump tump)
164.5 FX: gyu (shove)

166.2 FX: Baa (beep)
FX: Gatan gatan (clack clack)

167.1 FX: Kacha kacha (rattle rattle)
FX: Dota dota dota (thud thud thud)
167.5 FX: Don don ban (bang bang bam)

EDITOR'S RECOMMENDATIONS

The Ways People (and Things) Talk

Hotohori is the man in Hong-Nan with perhaps the best education and the worst social life. Never really having any friends his age (and his brothers were murdered in the internal strife that brought him to the throne), he's had to grow up among tutors, and that background has to come through in English as well as it does in the Japanese book. So the translation staff went out of their way to figure out just how Hotohori would speak if he were trying to impress the only people he saw on a daily basis, and that means using words that impress professors. Thus, you get Hotohori's affected speech and his use of the "royal we" when he acts as emperor. But you'll notice that those affectations and his use of "we" breaks down when he's alone with Miaka—the real Hotohori forces itself out into the open.

The "voice" of the text sections of *The Universe of the Four Gods* was tricky. How do you get across the feel of an ancient romantic epic without making it sound like corny Shakespeare imitations? At one point, someone in the translation team thought of using the style of Jane Austen (*Pride and Prejudice*, *Sense and Sensibility*)! It's familiar, understandable, and we don't have to use those pesky thees and thous! So the team started a reading marathon of Jane Austen works (the movies don't immerse you in the language enough), until Austen's speaking style was second nature (and pretty annoying to those in the office who had to hear it). And the product is what you can read in Volume 1 of *Fushigi Yûgi*!

Bill Flanagan
Editor of *Fushigi Yûgi*

Did you like *Fushigi Yûgi*? Here's what VIZ recommends you try next:

ALICE 19TH is Yû Watase's recent series about a seemingly normal teenage girl. One day, Alice hears strange voices telling her to save a rabbit. She almost loses her life rescuing the bunny, and soon finds out it's a magical entity with great powers that has a special message for Alice.

CERES: CELESTIAL LEGEND is an engaging story of love, betrayal and revenge by *Fushigi Yûgi*'s creator Yû Watase. Aya's world is turned upside when her family tries to kill her on her sixteenth birthday because of her family's deep, dark secret.

REVOLUTIONARY GIRL UTENA draws the reader into the world of a princess who wants to become a prince, just like the man who saved her as a little girl. Seven years later while trying to find the prince who rescued her, Utena finds out things are not as they appear and is forced to fight duels for the power to revolutionize the world.

Heaven Is About to Become Hell On Earth
Ceres Celestial Legend
The fate of a legend is redefined in this exciting conclusion to the anime series! From the creator of Fushigi Yûgi and based on the best-selling manga—now available from VIZ!
• Exclusive sleeve illustration from creator Yû Watase
• Features never before seen Yû Watase interview
• Collector's Edition, Volume 1: Reincarnation and Collector's Edition, Volume 2: Ascension — now available
Each volume includes 12 Episodes, 2-Discs $49.98!
Special Offer!
Buy Ceres Collector's Edition and get one of two FREE* limited edition display boxes!
* By mail. Must send proof-of-purchase and original store receipt, with shipping and handling.
©Yuu Watase / Shogakukan • Bandai Visual • Studio Pierrot. All rights reserved.
DVD VIDEO
shôjo
VIZ
www.viz.com